RENEWING EDUCATION

Selected Writings
by
Francis Edmunds

Hawthorn Press
Stroud

Published by Hawthorn Press, Bankfield House, 13 Wallbridge, Stroud GL5 3JA, UK

British Library Cataloguing in Publication Data
Edmunds, Francis
Renewing Education: Selected Writings by Francis Edmunds
I. Title
371.3

ISBN 1 869 890 31 0

Typeset by Bookman Ltd, Bristol
Printed by Billing and Sons Ltd, Worcester

Preface

When these essays (with the exception of one) were written between 1941 and 1958 the educational climate was very different from that of today. It was a critical time bridging the pre- and post-war periods, when ideas about education were being reviewed and the need to enlarge its scope was manifested in the 1944 Education Act. Selection procedures from primary to secondary education were based on the view that intelligence is measurable and that each person has his quota which can be permanently quantified in the early years by testing. In spite of this emphasis on intellectual capacity, the development of the imagination, the role of Art in education, and character-building as an essential part of schooling were themes whose importance was widely recognized among enlightened educators. The so-called progressive schools (among which Steiner Schools, also known as Waldorf Schools, were usually placed) were often the carriers of new educational ideas.

Since then the educational climate has changed considerably. In the UK state schools, and in some continental countries, egalitarianism established itself as a guiding principle. Equality of opportunity based on equal distribution of resources was to determine the structure of 'comprehensive' schooling from the 1960s on.

We are now in a third post-war phase. Education is now reified. It deals in things which are quantifiable. It is not the innate ability of the student which is measured but the product he or she carries off. The UK government is increasingly asserting itself as the directing force. Technology plays an accelerating role in the educational process, offering programmes to be purchased, determining assessment procedures, and threatening a further depersonalization of schooling.

From 1932 Francis Edmunds was a teacher in Michael Hall, a Rudolf Steiner School in Sussex. Later he established an Adult Education Centre nearby at Emerson College where he was active until his death in 1989. These essays on a considerable diversity of subjects are the fruits of his own experience as a teacher. Whether the subject is literature, science or religion there is always an enthusiastic search for the essence of the subject which educates. 'Education should be the greatest art of all, calling out a better form of manhood' writes Edmunds. Perhaps these words were more audible in the 1940s. Today, are they not more necessary? The theme at the heart of the following pages is that education must always join what we learn about the world with our inner human life. 'Science in our schools should bring man closer to an understanding of his own humanity.' In reality, science teaching usually serves only to distance the inner life of the child from the external world. The mood of contemporary culture is anti-idealistic and some people may therefore find themselves at odds with the unequivocal idealism of the author. Yet without ideals education must perish. Each age has to bring to expression its own deepest knowing. The attentive reader who is concerned about the decline in culture and education will find here either a challenging assault on his view point or a stimulating discovery of new perspectives. For those already familiar with Steiner education these essays offer fresh inspiration to its practice and understanding.

John Thomson
Emerson College 1991

Contents

Preface   iii

Contents   v

Acknowledgements   vii

Francis Edmunds   1

The Call   4

Questions from Mexico on Rudolf Steiner Education . . .   7

Eight Years with the Same Class Teacher   22
(from *Child and Man* (1951) Vol. 2, no. 6)

Religion, Art and Science   29
(from the *Michael Hall Journal* (1941) September,
October issues)

Feeling in the Growing Child   40
(from *Child and Man* (1952) Vol. 3, no. 3)

The Death of Baldur and the Festival of Resurrection . .   51
(from *Child and Man* Vol. 3, no. 2 (undated series))

Animal Teaching in the Fourth Class   71
(from *Child and Man* Vol. 3, no. 3 (undated series))

The First Approach to Physics   87
(from *Child and Man* (1950) Vol. 2, no. 1)

The Teaching of Religion at a Rudolf Steiner School . . .   95
(from *Child and Man* (1951) Vol. 2, no. 4)

Eighteen – The School Leaving Age 104
(from *Child and Man* (1954) Vol. 3, no. 8)

Teacher, Doctor and Farmer 110
(from the book *Tomorrow's Agriculture*)

Acknowledgements

The Publisher wishes to acknowledge the following.

The family of the late Francis Edmunds for their helpful assistance and support. Permission to reproduce 'The Call' and 'Questions from Mexico on Rudolf Steiner Education' from the private papers of Francis Edmunds is gratefully acknowledged.

Emerson College for permission to print an edited version of Georg Locher's funeral address from the Emerson College Newsletter, *Circles* (Spring 1990).

The International Biodynamic Initiatives Group for permission to reproduce the article, 'Agricultural Tasks of Our Time' (entitled 'Teacher, Doctor and Farmer' in this book), from their publication, *Tomorrow's Agriculture . . . Are We Meeting the Challenge?* (1986).

The Rudolf Steiner Schools Fellowship of Great Britain, and Michael Hall School, Forest Row.

Francis Edmunds

Francis Edmunds was born on 30 March 1902 into an orthodox Jewish family in Russia. His childhood destiny led him at an early age to England, where he was to step away from his family blood ties and look to find his own independent identity and path of destiny. Yet, in his training as a medical student in London, he did not find the image of man he was searching for. Too young to be drafted into the First World War, and suffering at the loss of life of young friends and acquaintances, he interrupted his studies, and at the age of about 21 we see Francis back in Russia as part of a Quaker relief mission, often on horseback, distributing supplies to the starving and homeless peasants. Later we see him in the Lebanon teaching English and football to Arabs, and then at the International School in Geneva also directing Shakespeare.

Strong inner experiences guide him to find Rudolf Steiner's Anthroposophy. He goes to Dornach, enrolls in courses and there meets up with the first teachers of the new Rudolf Steiner School in London (now Michael Hall). He joins the school in Streatham, arriving like a fireball with new enthusiasms and new ways. He intends to finish his medical training but the urgent need for a Class 1 teacher settles his destiny with Steiner's educational impulse.

For almost thirty years before founding Emerson College we see him putting immense energy and dynamism into the development of Waldorf education, as a class teacher and then concentrating on teaching adolescents in the Upper School. During the Second World War, with Michael Hall evacuated to Minehead, he writes and edits the *Michael Hall News*, founds and guides the Steiner Schools Fellowship, and gives lectures to soldiers. As early as 1936 he is one of the teachers who starts the Michael Hall Teachers' Training Course, which started again after the Second World War and was later incorporated into Emerson College.

In the early fifties he began his annual travels, first to America and then to the Southern Hemisphere, helping to found and develop Waldorf schools and anthroposophical groups and centres. He was master teacher and inspirer, powerfully uniting in his work the three pillars of education: Religion, Science and Art.

At the age of 60 and after years of inner preparation, Francis was able to found Emerson College at Forest Row in the autumn of 1962. With his wife Elizabeth and other colleagues who joined the work he pioneered the Foundation Year, directed the Education Course and helped further courses and trainings to come into being. He wished the College with its teaching out of anthroposophy to be an adult learning community rather than an academic institution; he wished it to be strongly connected with the land, with the arts and crafts and with scientific research.

It soon became a place where the world began to meet – a world college meeting world needs, creating around the globe a human connectedness of alumni who, with what they had found at Emerson, could give new expression to their life's work on all the continents of the earth.

Francis was a person foremost of will and intuition. He mastered the fiery choleric temperament and impatience of his younger years and became a deeply compassionate listener and counsellor, as well as remaining the youthful, uplifting speaker who, often with down-to-earth humour, made the spirit a creative experience of the moment, right up to his last day. The future was always with him and around him. Living longer than his chosen successor as principal of the College, John Davy, he was always looking and searching, really beyond the end of this century, for the succession to the work he had started.

As the truly moral and Christian force he is, he will surely continue to pioneer the education needed in this epoch of evolution, albeit now from the other side. Here he will live on in the striving, teaching and work of his students and colleagues.

(An edited version of the funeral address given on 20 November 1989 by Georg Locher.)

The Call

The increasing pressures of life in this century since the First World War have vastly altered both the outer circumstances and the inner attitudes of people the world over. We find ourselves caught up in tensions and conflicts of every kind without any visible signs of genuine solution. No matter who the warring parties are, the same cry rings out for right, justice and freedom. Yet moral values appear to be sinking to conditions of unmitigated violence and hate, whilst offering to the individual every enticement for self-indulgence, sex, drugs, and whatever else.

This is the view that presents itself to our young as they emerge from the naiveté of childhood. How are they not to be sucked into the general turmoil and confusion with its lack of trust in one another, and will right and wrong become no more than interchangeable terms according to who pronounces them the loudest? Ambitions there are in plenty, but where are the native-born ideals to sustain the human race? Are ideals of living no more than fictions to bolster up our prides? Are they really no more than sublimated instincts to cover up the beast beneath? Are faith, hope, charity and love no more than unsubstantiated dreams? What, then, is there left to live by? What as educators and parents also do we offer our youth in terms that they can accept from us?

We have to learn where idealism and realism meet in human nature, how ideals are born of innate faculties no less real than outer forms, how these need to be recognized at their source, understood, and nurtured like everything else that has a claim to live.

Education today pays scant attention to this question of ideals, though mention is made of them in programmes calculated to

4

encourage young people to take up the teaching profession. Years in the classroom, however, can and do lead to disappointment, to disillusionment, to a life of mere routine following the prescribed requirements of some governing board. Practical training for efficiency is the stated objective. That, of course, is necessary and fully justified, but that alone comes to be deadly dull for the teacher as the years go by, and spreads a deadness in the classroom. Mechanical efficiency, however excellent, is always dead, but human efficiency should never be, least of all in education where it is the living intercourse between teacher and pupil which is the very lifeblood out of which to create a future.

We live in an age in which the very mention of ideals is likely to be greeted with scepticism if not with downright suspicion. How many countries are there today where the free-born utterance of ideals may be regarded as dangerous, disruptive and subversive to the dominant ideology which happens to rule? Ideals are too controversial. Viewed in terms of sympathy and antipathy, they certainly are. Therefore it is considered safest for education to confine itself to the so-called practical preparation for efficiency in a given employment.

Life, however, moves in polarities. It is beginning to be realized that efficiency alone cannot succeed. Life without ideals grows savourless and without meaning.

Life without an ennobling goal must sooner or later, to use the phrase of even an avowed sceptic, Julian Huxley, sink into apathy or despair. 'Evolution has grown conscious' is a familiar phrase. It means that further evolution here on earth is accessible only to man but it has to be consciously directed, a willed evolution. 'Steeply up or steeply down' was the final alternative expressed by H.G. Wells near the end of his life. But it rests with the human being to have the will to climb. Lack of individual initiative to carry life further, lack of confidence in one's own potentials, has led to the trend towards centralist governments, even to the term 'benevolent dictatorships', to instruct people from outside what they are allowed to think, say and do. This was the logical conclusion arrived at by writers such as Aldous Huxley in his *Brave New World*, George Orwell in *1984*, C.S. Lewis in his

Abolition of Man and *This Hideous Strength,* and others. These are no mere phantasies. They are a call for a new awakening to inner freedom and moral responsibility for the future.

It is here that the teacher meets his greatest challenge. Education should not be classed as a profession. Education in the truest sense is a *calling*. This entails devotion and sacrifice. We need to hear the *call* of the younger generations for a life that is worth living. Not to hear that call is to betray our holiest trust.

Questions from Mexico on Rudolf Steiner Education

The following questions, and Francis Edmunds' answers, are taken from his written records of two lectures he gave to parents and members of the public on 18 and 20 February 1958 at the inauguration of La Nueva Escuela (The New School) in Mexico City, Mexico's first Rudolf Steiner School.

Question. Why place in Mexico a school of the Waldorf type? Does this education impart some doctrine, be it Protestant or Catholic, or is it just a doctrine in itself, or is it absolutely free?

Answer. This type of education is built on a new conception of man and is therefore intended for man wherever he may be. Though of European origin, it has a world character. Just as schools have sprung up in the free countries all over Europe, in Great Britain and America and also in New Zealand and Australia, because men were looking for a new impulse in education, so out of the educational needs of Mexico it came about quite naturally that people wanted a school of this type in this country. The education imparts no doctrine, it is neither Protestant nor Catholic but serves the child in his different stages of development out of new insight into childhood needs. The basis is Christian but the education pays serious regard to all aspects of human culture. Experience has shown that old scholars from these schools develop their own thoughts and ideas in complete freedom when they go out into life.

7

Question. Is the type of education you cite in your lecture adaptable to the demands of the Latin temperament in view of the absolute failure of some foreign methods in our country. In the *Psychology of Education* of Le Bons, the example is given of the failure of the English system in India.

Answer. As indicated in the answer to the preceding question, this education is not based on a system but on a study of the child. All children build up their faculties in a definite progression. Naturally, there are differences in different peoples, but just because this education is universally human it is best able to adapt itself to such differences. In the example you quoted, a method belonging to a Western people was applied to an Eastern people, apparently unsatisfactorily. Waldorf education can be planted anywhere but it unfolds according to the conditions offered it. Even in the same country no two schools are quite alike, yet they are all unmistakably Waldorf schools. An Indian educator, a lady, once visited a Waldorf school in England. It was explained to her that part of the endeavour in our schools was to hold back a too-rapid intellectual development in order to enable the children to develop and carry further their own powers of imagination. The reply was interesting. The Indian lady said that if this education were taken to India the problem there would be just the reverse. It would have to be adapted in such a way that the over-abundance of native imaginative experience would need to be checked and the intellectual faculty fostered more strongly. She was quick to see that this education can be adapted according to specific need. How it will work out in Mexico only experience in Mexico can show.

Question. Why does this education ground itself on an optimistic premise of love?

Answer. By 'love' is not meant mere sentiment. Love is a creative power which can speak at every level of experience.

It is innate in man. Without love, man can never fulfill his nature truly. Therefore, there is no question here of optimism but of recognizing what is actually there basic in human nature, and the task of the educator is to allow this to grow towards its own fulfillment. Out of love there proceed other qualities such as reverence, appreciation of others, human responsibility in action, etc. These qualities are latent in man. The right conditions of education give them the best opportunity to declare themselves. No more than sun-warmth is an optimistic premise where life is concerned, no more is love an optimistic premise in regard to man.

Question. Would you say something about discipline and your attitude and thought relating thereto; for example, 'Spare the rod and spoil the child', and so on?

Answer. Discipline is a very subtle matter. As you know, the word includes the meaning of disciple. This points immediately to the kind of relationship that should exist between teacher and child or, for that matter, between parent and child also. There are two factors which are above all important. In my experience, problems of discipline do not normally arise if the child feels both understood and loved. These are really complementary. Where there is true understanding there is also love, and where there is genuine love there is also understanding. In our use of the term love there is nothing sentimental. We mean the capacity to enter into the other and to perceive and appreciate the hidden greatness that is there. Therefore, love also implies reverence and gentleness.

It must be remembered that just as any living organism depends for its welfare upon its physical environment, so the child, as regards what we have called his invisible nature, depends upon the environment which only human beings out of their humanity can provide. But further, to understand the child means also to know how to serve his needs, how to engage his interests by offering the right educational material, how to provide the right activities, make the right demands, and so on. If this is done, then the child feels inwardly satisfied and therefore grateful.

If in spite of this there are disciplinary difficulties, then it is essential to diagnose the cause just as one would in any other case of disturbance. There may be various causes. I can only give one or two instances.

There are children who insist on drawing attention to themselves even if it means making real nuisances of themselves. In most cases it will be found that such children suffer neglect in their homes – either lack of attention or lack of love, or both. In one way or another they suffer from a sense of insecurity and this drives them to assert themselves at all costs. Here the therapy is plain. Without the cooperation of the parents, what the teacher can do is limited. He can only try to compensate for a lack that should not be there. In some instances it has been possible to compose a play for the whole class. The particular child is given an appropriate role whereby his usual relationship with his fellows is totally altered. There have been instances where this has worked an amazing transformation.

I remember the case of a small boy who suffered through the death of his father. In addition, he had some severe operations which had left hard scars on his body. And further, he had gone to a school where from a young age he had been deliberately trained to be ambidextrous so that, in effect, he did not know his right hand from his left and was often in state of general confusion. He was both assertive and fearful. When he was about 9, the teacher had the idea of giving him the part of St. Christopher in a class play. It was astonishing to see this child grow into his part. Today he is a man and has himself become a teacher. It may be said that the Staff of St. Christopher has never left his hand.

A more obvious case is that of a rampageous boy who was pampered and spoiled and so felt himself to be no end of a lad. In showing off, he once broke something in a classroom through sheer abuse. On that occasion the woodwork teacher took the trouble to have this boy back at school regularly over a certain period of time. This in itself had an effect. The boy had to realize that the teacher's concern was so great that, in spite of being a busy man, he thought it worthwhile to punish himself for the sake of the boy. With the teacher's help the boy made a piece of furniture which was badly needed in that particular classroom. The day came when, without comment, it was put in position to serve the whole community of the class. This treatment too had an astonishing effect.

One could go on. The main point is that therapy is always constructive. Merely negative punishment, hundreds of useless lines for example, which cost the teacher nothing, is useless.

Anger is sometimes well in place provided it is righteous anger over a given circumstance and not just personal outrage and resentment. There is about as little sense in a teacher growing furious over a child's disturbed condition as there would be in a doctor hurling a hammer at a patient's head because he had an awkward complaint.

In the last resort, in a Waldorf school, there are weekly meetings of teachers to discuss the children and therefore to arrive at a collective judgement and agreed therapy. In this way there is little room left for merely subjective attitude. True discipline is neither a code nor a system, neither coercive nor sentimentally lax – it is a human art, the starting point being love and understanding for the child.

Question. I would like to know if this type of education – in which the potentialities and the inner morality of the child are developed – will not result in difficulties on the part of the child in adjusting himself to the world around him where the majority of people have had a different education?

Answer. I will answer this question by a particular instance. It happened some years ago that I was present as a listener at a debate amongst old scholars of Michael Hall on the question, 'What has education done for us?'

There were various attempts at answers. It is naturally very difficult to determine to what extent a man's life has really been affected by his schooling. One knows oneself as one is and it is hard to imagine how one might have been different had one not gone to that particular school. Eventually one old scholar got up and said 'In my opinion, this education has made life much harder for me but I would not have missed this for worlds because it has taught me what real living means.'

Looking back over the years I find that our old scholars are markedly individual. They go about life not with a set mode or philosophy but with an openness towards the world and the capacity to meet circumstances out of their own resources. If we educate rightly, the resulting individual should be in better command of his own capacities and should be better able to draw his own conclusions. Speaking generally, our old scholars are interested in life, in situations, above all in people different from themselves. Out of their interest, they develop initiative and are rarely content to stay put. Because they feel the problems of others, they also feel the necessity to try and intervene helpfully and to take on responsibilities which may bring burdens but which constitute real life. I think this is what that particular old scholar meant.

Question. At what age should we put our children to school?

Answer. I would say, in theory, that if the home is the right sort of home where, for example, there is one's own house and garden, where Dad comes and does things and Mother is busy and there is time for the child to enjoy both and to delight in being busy alongside Dad and Mum – where these ideal circumstances obtain, there is no need for the child to go school until he is ready to enter the school proper at 6. Until then I believe that home life provides the ideal schooling. But also, in modern times and under modern conditions where is such home life to be found? Therefore, the nursery school and the kindergarten are there to compensate for what the home now rarely provides. There the children find companionship and occupation of the right kind – opportunities to imitate what goes on in the big adult world.

At Michael Hall we take children from the age of 4. Some

of our nursery schools take them from the age of 3. I think it a tragedy if children are sent off even earlier than that.

In any case, under no circumstances should formal education be encouraged before the age of 6 or, more properly, before the change of teeth.

Question. What happens if the child transfers to another school?

Answer. Again I would like to answer this question with a particular instance. Michael Hall, before the Second World War, was in London. It had then about 300 children. War broke out during the summer vacation when many of the children were scattered over the countryside. The school had quickly to be evacuated to the West of England. When the children were finally assembled, we found we had lost 100 of them ranging in age through all the school years. We had good opportunities for following up some of them. The general pattern was the following. Since we do not drive our children intellectually in the earlier years and since, in any case, our curriculum is much wider than in most schools and the approach less academic, there was, in every case, a period of adjustment during which some of our children seemed to be at a disadvantage. Then, however, their freshness and liveliness of interest began to assert itself and from then on they began to go ahead surprisingly. Children who, in our estimation, had seemed average stood out in their new surroundings.

I can also quote the experiences of the Rudolf Steiner School in New York City. For many years, until quite recently, it was an elementary school only. Children had to leave at the end of the eighth grade, but they often did so from the seventh and even from the sixth grades to make sure of gaining entry to their selected schools. The record over the years was greatly encouraging. Almost without exception these children did very well and seemed often to surpass themselves. The reason is the same as that already quoted. This education releases capacities, keeps the mind and imagination fresh and awakens life interests. These qualities the children take with them wherever they go, making the transfer not only possible but mostly very successful. The same applies to entry to life.

Question. I should like to know something about the teacher –child relationship carried on for eight years continuously.

Answer. This is a vast question and could be answered in many ways. As I have said, we discriminate between three distinct phases of childhood – the pre-dentition years, the elementary school years, and the adolescent years. It may be said that in the first phase the child is mainly concerned with throwing off what is mere heredity and in preparing his own body as an instrument for life. It may equally be said that in the adolescent phase the young person is mainly concerned with establishing his own personal relationship to his environment. Real childhood belongs to the middle phase and this should be seen as one continuous period carrying over from the spontaneous childhood phantasy and imitative play of the earlier years to the birth of the critical faculty and the thoughtful discrimination which arises in the later years. Of course, no phase begins or ends abruptly. Therefore, the eight intervening years which make up the class-teacher period resolve themselves, broadly speaking, into three lesser phases. The imitative period lingers on decreasingly until about the ninth year when there is a definite psychological change, a jump in self-awareness. At the opposite end, adolescence throws its shadow back to a pre-adolescent stage commencing at about the twelfth year when there is equally a marked change in mental and emotional response. Since life, also in its moral aspects, is organically continuous, it is the task of the class teacher to carry over the earlier conditions into the later ones in the most harmonious manner possible. Also, in these formative years the child reveals not only capacities but inner hindrances. The former needs to be encouraged, the latter to be overcome, and for this to be effective it is necessary to live in continuous connection not only with the child but with the home, for in various ways and at different times, consultation and cooperation between the class teacher and the parents becomes quite essential. All this gives an established center to the child's life as he moves between parent and teacher and lives within the community of his class. Within the whole group of children also, there will be many social adjustments which need to be fostered and helped as a vital part of the social education of the child.

There is the natural fear that there might arise an unhappy relationship between a teacher and a member of his class, the perpetuation of which over a period of years might prove disastrous. Actually, because the work is conducted at a highly objective level through the close and constant cooperation of the whole teacher body, the danger of this is almost entirely eliminated. I can recall only one or two instances over a period of more than twenty-five years when serious difficulties arose and these were found to emanate from a lack of confidence between the parents and the teacher which then involved the child. The overall advantages have been proved beyond doubt in the course of nearly forty years of experience in many schools in many lands.

It should be remembered, of course, that right from the first grade on, the children have several teachers apart from the class teacher. The class teacher has the Main Lesson subjects. He is the central authority, assisted by the other teachers who take languages, music, eurythmy, handicrafts, and so on.

Question. Why does the child in his instinctive observation always bring forth in his representative images the brightest of colours? Red, for example.

Answer. It is not so that all children bring forth the brightest of colours. Some may produce dirty and inharmonious colours. The fact is that the younger the child, the more does he put onto paper, free from mental reflection, a true and immediate expression of himself. A child in good health will produce, if given the opportunity, pure and beautiful colours. A child who is physically ill or nervously disturbed will produce jarring and disturbed effects. A choleric child delights in bright reds. A melancholic child is more likely to enjoy blues and purples. Some people paint gently, even faintly, others crassly. The work a child does spontaneously is a marvellous guide to an understanding of the child himself. There have been many instances where, by helping a child to overcome ugly and discordant forms and colours, the whole child has achieved greater harmony and sense of well-being.

Question. Would you be so kind as to specify, to some extent at least, the infantile psychological characteristics and the way of applying this in the period of primary studies?

Answer. The dominant characteristic of the child in the pre-school years is that of imitation. The child imitates all that is in his environment, not only the obvious things but what lives as attitude of mind and heart in the adult. Therefore, the responsibility of the adult is to strive in every way to be a worthy example, in his own human outlook and behaviour and also in his whole way of conduct, for imitation. Every child has a feeling of dependence on the adult and this, in the elementary school years, takes the form of a longing for true authority. By this is not meant mere formal outer control, but authority through faith in the teacher and what he brings forward because he is wise enough to understand what the child really needs. When what is offered to the child does not correspond to his needs, problems of discipline are bound to arise. Right example and right understanding produce right authority.

We are not here considering *problem* children.

Question. You say that the child in his first school (that is, in the first five years) finds a deep joy. Is this due to the joy of companionship or of discovery in the environment?

Answer. Joy is to a young child what sunshine is to a flower. It has an expanding quality which strengthens the will and invokes courage and enthusiasm. The child will naturally find deep joy in the companionship of adults where there is genuine love and understanding. Equally, the child will find joy when experiences coming from the environment call to what is wanting to declare itself in the child. In this respect, there can be serious error. We have to distinguish between joy and mere fascination. So much that is offered the child today in the way of toys, for example, is merely clever. The dressed-up doll that can be undressed and that performs tricks may for the moment absorb the child, but leaves no room for his own active fantasy. A far simpler toy with which the child can really play and create gives more real joy and educationally is far more valuable.

Question. Why is it desirable to have the same class teacher for six or eight consecutive years? Wouldn't the children's personalities benefit from knowing different teachers with different characters?

Answer. The fact that a child has the same class teacher does not mean at all that he does not meet other teachers. He has teachers for languages, for music, for arts and crafts as they are developed, for eurythmy, for gymnastics, and so on. The class teacher is the central guide through the elementary school years and is concerned with the presentation of the main cultural subjects, given in block periods during the morning main lesson which lasts approximately two hours. Childhood is a continuous process. The child may have difficulties which require years to resolve. The child may have latent faculties which require care and understanding if they are to be developed. A child has health problems or temperamental difficulties which need to be followed up. Above all, the child in the early years needs a focus to his life which guarantees stability and security. The class teacher is able to follow these matters stage by stage, and to adapt his work to the gradual change from early childhood fantasy to the beginnings of intellectual thought. During these transition years which are so profoundly formative, the class teacher is able to maintain a continuous connection with the home so that home and school may cooperate to the best advantage.

Moreover, the class teacher maintains connection with all the other teachers concerned with the child so that there is a continuous overall study and survey. Because this education is not based on merely personal values but on a real study of man in which all the teachers in a Waldorf school participate, the work is carried at a level which precludes small and petty likes and dislikes. In the experience of many years in many schools, there have been only rare instances of a serious clash between a class teacher and a particular child, and even then it has generally proved to be due to a lack of confidence and cooperation between the parents and that particular teacher.

By contrast, we may ask what can it mean in a child's life if, year after year, he has to adapt himself to a totally new personality and if the teachers, receiving new groups of children each year, have to try and learn to know those children sufficiently in so short a time in order to be able to give them the most vital help they need. It is an almost impossible task if we are thinking in terms of real child development and not merely of scholastic records. A child needs, above all, to be understood and this requires time and continuity, and a sense of secure anchorage in these early years. Emancipation from class-teacher authority comes naturally with adolescence. Then, what has been built up in these years translates itself into self-reliance and inner security.

Question. What is the positive effect of the impression of the fairy tale fantasy on the child?

Answer. The true fairy tale comes down to us from a time when human beings had not yet developed the critical intellectual faculties on which we depend so much today. There was a fund of natural wisdom handed down from generation to generation, containing wonderful secrets of life in picture form. Once we begin to study the fairy tale seriously, we may soon discover what profound meaning is contained there, and this speaks to the child and nurtures him even as it did the peoples of old. All true fairy tales end positively, for example in 'They lived happily ever after', because of a profound faith that whatever trials life might present, ultimately they will be resolved for good. Fairy tales comprise a language of the imagination. The child responds naturally and discriminates in his feelings between the good and the bad, the beautiful and the ugly, the true and the false, thus educating his heart judgement for life. This later becomes clear insight.

Question. Could you tell me the degree of educative perception in the child of 12 years and through what faculties does he relate himself to the world around him?

Answer. Generally speaking, there are definite signs of psychological change around the twelfth year. The child is then at the dawn of the approach to puberty and with that there comes a more thoughtful and conscious questioning of the world around him. But this, however, is not to be confused with actual adolescence, though unhappily this confusion exists very widely. The child at 12 still longs for true authority and still lives more in his heart-feeling qualities of judgement than in his mental-critical attitude. Lack of understanding of this is one of the chief causes of disturbance in childhood today. *Children are approached with adult attitudes far too soon.* This danger is mitigated in a Waldorf school where due allowance is made for the period between pure childhood ending at about 12 and the birth of the true adolescent at about 14 or 15.

Question. As the mother of an adolescent who still has made no decision of a road in life, how can I know when to leave him free for choice of action and decision?

Answer. Briefly, all young people still need guidance and are glad to receive it if it comes to them in a right form. The responsibility of the adult does not cease. It is only a question of adjusting the relationship between the adult and the child. As the child enters into adolescence, the strong nature bond of the early years of childhood should grow weaker, to be replaced by a steady strengthening of what may be termed companionship through understanding. Where this has been cultivated and maintained, there should be no serious problem, for it is then a matter of joint concern, study and inquiry between child and parent as to what the next step in life can best be. Two dangers threaten – one is that the child is too soon treated as an adult; the other is that the adolescent is too long regarded as merely a child.

Question. What can I do with a child who is slightly retarded mentally?

Answer. Distinction must be made between the slow-developer who is a perfectly normal child and the child who is mentally retarded. In a Waldorf school we discriminate between children who may be over-sleepy, children who are healthily dreamy, and children who are over-wakeful. Often the sleepy child actually needs to sleep longer and resists intellectual activity because he has greater powers which need to slumber longer. Some outstanding leaders have been slow developers. Treatment of such children falls naturally within the scope of class teacher work. Real mental retardation requires special measures, special activities, greater emphasis on rhythm and repetition, and so on. In both cases, results will be achieved not by dinning at the head but by working patiently from the limbs up. It will be a question of careful consultation to decide what the state of the child really is. In Europe and Great Britain there are schools where Waldorf methods have been adapted for children in need of special care. It is to be hoped that such schools will also find their way into Mexico one day.

Question. Even if it were possible to start every child of school age at the present time with a Waldorf school education, in how many generations could we overcome inherited tendencies and the influence of adults not so educated?

Answer. This education is born of our times to meet the needs of our times. Every child that benefits brings a positive gain to the community. We can only work in this sense.

Question. What are the preventative methods of avoiding child delinquency in the large cities? In what way can we avoid juvenile delinquency?

Answer. This is far too big a question to be answered briefly. There is no doubt, however, that much juvenile delinquency is due to frustration and lack of regard to the real needs of the child. Often there is a lack of love in the initial stages, bad example, pampering or denial, no adequate appeal to fantasy and imagination – in fact, subconsciously the child feels that his essential being has been neither understood nor truly received into life. There is no doubt that within the methods of Waldorf education there live very largely the conditions which can counter and heal delinquent tendencies.

Eight Years
with the Same Class Teacher

The work of the class teacher forms the heart and centre of the life of a Rudolf Steiner School. This has often been said. Whatever may be new in other ways in a Rudolf Steiner School, the class teacher with his or her span of eight years is the greatest innovation of all. The idea that one teacher should be responsible for the same group of children uninterruptedly for so long a time comes as a surprise. In practice it has proved to be most natural and deeply satisfying. Whoever has once had this experience must quail at the thought of working differently. If continuity is desirable in other spheres of work, it is surely most desirable in this one, for what can require more continuous care and nursing than the human being in the tender years from 6 to 14, from the early stage of lisping childhood, with its unconscious devotion to adult guidance and authority, to the birth of the somewhat unruly, perhaps cantankerous and argumentative, and yet equally devoted and now consciously seeking young adolescent?

What can compare with these eight years of intimate tutelage? The class teacher stands there surrounded by his group of growing children, himself supported by the circle of his colleagues within the school and by the wider circle of his parents outside. His responsibility is a heavy one for he knows that in these impressionable years his influence is immense and goes very deep. In term time and in holiday time his children are ever with him. Whatever else he may be doing, his thoughts turn ever and again to them. Each year, each season indeed, brings its special opportunities and these must be recognized, held and applied, for they will not come again in the same form. If a child has gifts he must discover them and help them forward. If a child has difficulties he must see them, understand them, and work unremittingly to try to resolve them.

He knows his children must one day leave him. For him that day is one of heavy reckoning. What little has he really been able to accomplish for the one or the other child? How much must he sadly admit to have left undone? No one knows better than he does his own shortcomings, and the more accomplished and capable the teacher, the more will this be true for him. How will his children shape in the remaining years in the Upper School? How will they enter life? After all, this education has aims that go far beyond immediate requirements.

There is, however, mercy as well as justice. As his children, now grown to manhood and womanhood, seek him out in later years, with powers to recall and to form their own judgement, seeing him now adult to adult, he may find comfort and consolation in the shy devoted friendship that streams to him from them. They have learnt to know him as the friend who stood by them in their most helpless and dependent years, working for them to the best of his abilities, and they are grateful. They may begin to assess for themselves the nature of the help they received and to understand why things took the course they did. Long years afterwards the 'meaning' may flash in upon their souls of something they once received in childhood, and if their hearts can ring to it, it will be a moment of great joy. Then their childhood, as Rudolf Steiner once described it, will be like a summertime within them, warming, blessing, and renewing them in later life.

The above may be taken as describing facts that have been proved and experienced many and many a time since this education was first introduced over thirty years ago. Teachers and old scholars can testify to its truth. The details, the personal colourings, may be different in each case but the main bearing on life is strikingly the same. For the class teachers in the one or in the different schools, in the one or in the different lands, have the same ideals, the same vision of childhood and of growing manhood; they have the same role to play of protecting friend and pastor; they draw their wisdom and their inspiration from a common source, the new knowledge about man given to the world in this century by Rudolf Steiner. They strive to be artists in their work, knowing that art rules without dogma and works and influences others through the free acceptance of what it has to give. Art for the class teacher covers life itself. If the teacher is an artist in his nature, then whatever he may be called upon to do with his children and for his children, he will guide them without compulsion and according to their actual needs. This is the deepest secret of the class teacher's calling, that he seeks above all to be an artist in his method. His art of teaching will then have, like every art, healing as its goal. Only a healthy soul can have a right enjoyment of life. It is not, however, a question just of enjoyment, whether of work or of pleasure. Great art aims further, it aims to waken in man forces of reconciliation with his destiny as man, forces that can release him from the unavoidable circumstances of everyday mundane living because they give him an inner vision of ennoblement and of higher manhood. Such influences work slowly but they work surely. They do not divorce men from everyday realities but they bring a greater reality to bear on everyday life; for what reality can there be in life unless men are filled with a sense of progress towards higher goals – in its final statement, towards God.

We live in prosaic times, overshadowed by every kind of fear. The very use of the word 'ideal' today provokes scepticism and doubt. Thus also, the role of the class teacher may appear to be so ideal as to be quite impracticable. The above description must inevitably call up many questions. Where can we find such perfect men and women? What if the teacher should fall short – is not then the whole system condemned outright? Is not the risk far too great and is it not better, in that case, to keep to the usual, less ideal, arrangement of having a different class teacher each year – then, at least, the good teachers may partly cancel out the bad? And have not teachers the common failings of other folk, weaknesses, indiscretions, favouritisms, pet aversions and the like? And what if a child should dislike his class teacher – is it not a fearful punishment to have to endure him for eight whole years, and might it not bring disastrous effects for the whole of life?

These are very real questions and they cannot be glossed over. They may, however, be turned the other way. In nineteen years of teaching in a Rudolf Steiner School I have never known of a relationship between a class teacher and a child that failed or broke down. Even where children, especially as they approach 13 or 14, have appeared to be critical, at the moment of parting from their class teacher their real love for him has shown itself unmistakably. There have been sad instances when a class teacher has had to give up; together with his colleagues he had to come to the sad admission that, for health or other reasons, he lacked the powers necessary for his task. Such a situation does arise occasionally and it always entails deep suffering for everyone concerned, but it has never arisen, to my knowledge, through bad human relationships. Judged by ordinary standards this must seem a strange and unlikely statement. How are we to account for it?

The answer is to be sought partly in the nature of the work and partly in the organization of the school. What is required of a Rudolf Steiner School teacher? He must, like other teachers, have knowledge, abilities, life experience. These, however, will not suffice; he must also be prepared to work at himself. His work, as has already been said, is based on a new study of man – man as being of body, soul and spirit. In the light of this teaching there is no room for chance and caprice. Whatever the human being reveals of good and of bad must be taken seriously. Responsibility towards man lives first and foremost in his soul. This new study can never remain merely theoretical. It calls for action, for practice and, above all, for a training in self-knowledge. The only guide to a knowledge of others is through a knowledge of self. Through self-knowledge the teacher acquires a right humility towards his own abilities because he discovers his own limitations; he cannot come right with his task unless he is prepared to grapple with his limitations and to try to overcome them. This is the opposite of introspection which leads a man merely to an unhealthy brooding over his insufficiencies. The teacher cannot paint with his children unless he himself works in colour. The moment he begins to do so he encounters difficulties and he will gladly turn to others who may help him. The same is true of all his work.

More than all this, however, is the problem of how to be truly a man. More important than any gifts the teacher may possess, says Rudolf Steiner, is what he himself *is*. The teacher knows as he stands before his children that he himself is being judged at every moment. The children have a right to expect of him that he should be a true representative for them of the best forces in manhood. This is a hard fact to be faced but he must do so. If, however, he can find the necessary courage to face himself he may in that moment begin to discover in himself the true charity of heart for others, the kind of charity or love of which St. Paul speaks. Such love can only come with self-knowledge. It is never sentimental, can never pick and choose, and is least of all concerned with personal likes and dislikes. It makes men conscious and therefore capable. It acts as pure light and sun-warmth on the soul of childhood. This love the teacher must possess. It is a love than can grow, giving him eyes and ears for the needs of his children. Such a teacher, even should he make mistakes, will surely be forgiven, and he in turn will be loved by his children. Without this love between the consciously striving adult and the unconsciously aspiring children, the classroom is a desert place. No amount of cleverness and of external efficiency can alter this fact.

And thus it comes about that preparation for a Steiner School teacher involves something quite special. Each day he meets his children. Each night he thinks about them. He reviews what has gone by and prepares for the next day. As he thinks of his children he thinks also of their parents and he mounts in prayerful thought to those powers who have yet to be made manifest in them. His preparation is not just a matter of covering a given syllabus, though this too should not be neglected. He has constantly to find the right material and the right method of presentation to serve the purely human needs of his children. He must carry the class forward as a whole – but the class consists of single children. What verse can help the one, what exercise the other, what story a third? If, to take but one example, his class should be in its fourth

year, the curriculum recommends the Norse stories. Looking at
the individual children he will be able to determine which stories
to select and how best to narrate them, for the choleric child,
the phlegmatic child, the dreamy child, the nervous child, and
so on. His object is to help where help is needed. Should he
decide to write a play, his thoughts will most likely turn first to
his 'difficult' children, one who is perhaps too timid, another who
is too uncontrolled, a third who unhappily is a kind of Cinderella
in the class. How can he, by means of a play, help to bring these
children into a right social relationship with the others. He must,
however, keep a clear eye for the 'easy' children too, those who
learn eagerly and quickly, who are by nature social and generally
popular – for, should he fail them in their needs, they too will
begin to show difficulties. Thus he must be watchful of all and
of each, and his eye must carry his heart within it. Under these
circumstances there is little enough room for petty differentations,
for personal likes and dislikes. The work is lifted to another level,
we might also say a Christian level.

Another important factor in a Steiner School which protects
the work, helping teacher and children alike, is the co-operation
within the College of Teachers. Such a College is not constituted
arbitrarily but has deep social roots.

In no school has the single teacher more scope and freedom
for his work. On the other hand, problems that arise are brought
to the weekly meeting of the College of Teachers. Of course,
teachers consult one another at all times according to need. But
this weekly meeting draws the whole life of the school together
and the children are discussed. The same child may be seen in his
different activities and through the eyes of several teachers and
from this comprehensive view a common judgement is sought.
Sometimes it is the class teacher who brings up a child; at other
times it may be another teacher after consultation with the class
teacher. All the acquired knowledge, wisdom and experience
possessed by the whole body of teachers can thus be focused on
a single point. In this way, onesidedness in judgement is quickly
eliminated. Such discussions based on a child's work, behaviour,
appearance, health, unexpected change of circumstance, bring

mutual enlightenment to the teachers, and they also have a remarkable effect on the child. It is common knowledge in Steiner Schools that often after a serious discussion about a child there is a visible improvement the following morning. Discussion alone is obviously not sufficient; it should be an incentive to further observation and to work. Nevertheless, it is well known among Steiner teachers that through such discussions something often takes effect which is more than can be due to the sum total of the abilities of the teachers present. Where there is a sincere striving for truth, a sincere regard for the being of the child and a longing to help him, grace and power may flow into such a discussion; there comes moments when a kind of wonder breaks in upon those who are present so that the experience of the words 'where two or three are gathered together in My name . . .' draws very near. That this should be the case is the highest ideal of the work of a College, or a Community, of Teachers in a Steiner School, in this there lives the greatest protection of all both for teacher and for child.

Religion, Art and Science

Tolstoy wrote a pamphlet, 'What is Religion?'. He also wrote a book, *What is Art?*. He never seems to have asked 'What is Science?' In this respect he was quite modern. It would hardly occur to anyone today to ask 'What is Science?' for it is self-evident. On the other hand, we might very well ask 'What is Art?'

Art would always refer us to something which is not obvious but which may be discovered. Does that something belong to an objective world, or is it a purely subjective impression? If it is an objective world, then we ask 'What world?' If it is a subjective impression, then we ask 'What is the subject?'

Religion has become very much a question for great numbers of people. Religion must pre-suppose an invisible creator; in the West this creator has become a personal God. It is based on articles of faith; its basis can never be imparted as knowledge for it has no ground of proof. How many ingenious theories there are explaining away the origin of religion; merely proving to those who are religious-minded that the theorists lack something? On the other hand, how very theoretical is every attempt to explain religious experience? It seems as though one has it or one has it not. Again, religious experience and religious faith are not at all one and the same thing, for religious experience includes all the known 'faiths' of humanity. A Buddhist, a Moslem or a Jew can be equally as religious as a Christian – they all look from this world to another; but how differently! Art stands before us to appreciate or not; it makes itself evident to the senses though the senses alone cannot grasp it. Religion is completely hidden.

But a few centuries ago in the world's history the matter was quite different. Science was not at all common knowledge; for

29

the greater part of mankind it was a mystery, regarded even
with suspicion. So long as it remained in the realm of Natural
Philosophy – that is, of Ideas – it could be tolerated, though even
then it lent itself easily to the charge of heresy; the moment it
dabbled in 'experiment' it became 'black magic'. Roger Bacon's
experiments would appear child's play to the average schoolboy
of 15, but on their account he spent long years in prison and was
always under grave suspicion.

On the other hand, in those days it was art that was self-evident
– so much so that it was never questioned. There was no Theory
of Art – no Science of Aesthetics. There were the great individual
artists and there was popular art in every shape and form, above
all in handicrafts. There was always that something extra beyond
the merely utilitarian which made the works of man beautiful.
It came so naturally that men did not talk of it in terms of art
at all – it simply had to be. In those days men could never
have argued about the existence of the soul for it was more
obvious and real than sense-life itself and it poured itself into
that something extra that made a door-hinge or a chimney-corner
beautiful. Because this was so, religion also had a natural place
in human life and could not be questioned. That which fills
us with amazement in the details of every old church came
about not 'consciously' but as natural process. Men fashioned
as they felt and large communities could feel in common even
as we today can think in common. Religion was the ground of
common feeling. Nevertheless, it was a mystery; it was felt as a
birth within the soul but it was no more obscure than ordinary
birth. Today even people in the same church and congregation
feel differently about religion; there are fundamental differences
in point of view. Then, religion was the common experience of
the whole community differing in individuals only in degree. In
the enactment of the mass the whole congregation felt exalted,
was lifted out of ordinary bodily experience and men knew one
another united in a higher experience; for the time being they
were 'changed' and they felt this change permeating the rest
of their daily life. The power of the Word, for that exalted
moment, spoke directly to the heart and not via the head, all

the more so because the Word was in Latin and not understood – indeed, the not understanding was important for it excluded all possibility of a mere head relationship. Something flowed like a 'Presence' into the assembly and it made itself felt as a life-force, a renewing force, not 'understood' but more real than anything that could be understood – hence the mystery. After all, the child does not need to 'understand' in order to experience vitality, and blessed is the adult who has retained even to a faint degree this superabundant life-force and intensity of experience of the child; it is this very force, carried into mature years, that we recognize in the human genius.

This then was a time when science was commonly unknown; when art was self-evident as common experience subjectively expressed – just as science is today; and when religion and not the sensibly perceived was felt to be the ground of all existence. This condition persisted for long periods of time for the different peoples of the world; the further we go back, the more nearly do we find art related to religion – so that art is the veil of religious experience – till, finally, art in outer form also disappears and we have only religion permeating every aspect of life.

Nothing is left of the most ancient periods of Indian and Persian culture except a few holy verses written down many centuries later, not because men were less creative in those distant times – men have always been creative for that is the distinctive mark of man – but because inward experience was so strong and so akin to actual perception of the spiritual that it was all-sufficient. Art expressed itself in one stupendous act – in the forming of society as a whole – and society was organized in every detail as a reflection of spiritual law. Authority lay with the seer who was at one and the same time the priest, the teacher, the legal adviser if not the actual legislator, the healer – the father of all. Hence the great reverence for the teacher that still lives in the East. We have only to think of the ancient caste system with its spiritual headship as the source of all direction for life. We meet this again in Zarathustra, in Moses, in Hermes and in the later Pharaohs or Priest-Kings. Society was fashioned into an artistic-social unity from a source that descended from the mountain heights of 'spirit-knowledge'.

Thus it was in the earliest times until, further back, we pass beyond the dim origins of historical consciousness into the purely mythical ages. In the mythologies we have portrayals of a time when the earthly processes themselves were experienced as spiritual events; life with all its manifold shapes and contours melts from view into an ever-present experience of the divine. In those unrecorded ages before the dawn of history one could not speak even of religion, for religion means to 're-unite', to 're-bind', and man was not yet completely sundered for a direct perception of the divine. Rudolf Steiner describes the earliest mythologies as dreams of the creation of the human body – spiritual aspects of bodily creation involving manifold activity on the part of 'higher beings' who were fulfilling their own destinies in the making of man. Then when the body was sufficiently fashioned in the 'image of God' – when man stood complete in the splendour of physical creation – from out of this 'body' there awoke 'religion' as natural revelation expressed in cult and ritual, in enactments on earth of the mysteries of 'pre-birth'. And then, when, long ages after, the soul had grown sufficiently with the body, there awoke as an after-echo of all that had gone before – expressing itself now through the capacities and deeds of individual men, and adapted now to earth existence – the various manifestation of Art. And finally, when the soul had so steeped itself in natural existence that it felt itself as one with its bodily nature, there awoke the further faculty, by slow degrees, of intelligence, of thought and understanding for the earth as such. Human, individual intelligence, capable, to begin with, of grasping the earthly nature only – the point where humanity as a whole stands today.

But now, with all this given, the eternal nature in man, come to its first degree of self-knowledge in the thinking being of man, must set out on its long journey of discovery – sweeping on from purely earthly experience at the level of the senses to the exercise of ever higher faculties of cognition. For the exercise of these higher faculties man is really only at the chrysalis stage; he is undergoing the entombment that must lead to reawakening.

Our vast edifice of material construction is the rock that must be moved before we can come to the first glimpse of the higher man in man. The suffering that is spread over the world on such a vast scale is the pain that must be borne if the will is to be so intensified that it can become equal to its task. Then the weight that bears us down will be changed into its opposite and we shall experience the 'lightness' of the gardener hovering over the flowers of the field as in the beautiful picture of Fra Angelico. The vision of the artist will become one day the direct seeing of the individual soul. Between the 'glad tidings' that heralded the Christ-child to earth, proclaimed by angels unto men, and the wondering gaze of the human soul on the morning of the resurrection, there lies a world of sorrows; but who would forego that sorrow knowing the event to come?

Science, art and religion have fallen apart for modern man, even as thought, feeling and will are no longer understood in their mutual relationships. When these grow, united again in human consciousness, even as head, heart, and limbs are part of one being, then Man will appear before us shining with the beauty of the Risen One. Our thinking will grow so much more virile that we shall hardly know it as thought for it will be like an awakening from sleep; our feeling, released from the nightmare of physical bondage will grasp existence in living imagination of spiritual being, and our will, now fettered by necessity, will develop wings that will lift it into the pure light of self-determined action united with the will of worlds. 'Thy will be done' will no longer mean passive resignation to a higher decree, but active and joyous acknowledgement in self-devotion to the highest.

We will now consider religion, art, and science in relation to the child life and to education.

Child life and Education

Having shown how religion, art and science are related to one another in the progressive history of mankind, we should expect, in so far as childhood is a spiritual-organic process recapitulating the past, to find a very special connection between Religion, Art and Science and the growing years of life.

We know that in the first seven years the main work of man is the perfecting of the physical organism. The physical model received from the parents is, in the course of these years, replaced by a new physical body, permeated through and through with the forces of the newly incarnating individuality. The main character of these years is expressed in the remarkable force of Imitation whereby alone the child can learn effectively from the surrounding world; how, in the plastic nature of the young child, this imitation through gesture – or in subtler forms, in breathing and sense-perception – works back upon the organism, implanting in the very organs themselves the predisposition for health or ill-health in later life, for strength of will and a harmonious sense of inner security in the midst of life or for ineffectiveness and a lack of confidence in oneself and in life as a whole. These first years are therefore of real importance for the whole of life and have an all-determining influence on the years to come. The good that is done will come as blessing and the harm as hindrance and difficulty for the adult. In these years, therefore, there is the greatest call from the child for the deepest moral forces in the adult, for the qualities of mercy, of reverence, of compassionate sympathy. These years, we might say, are in very truth the 'religious' years of childhood; not, of course, as creed, but as purest human experience. The very fact of the unlimited power of Imitation whereby the child learns his first adaptation to life implies for these years the character of faith, of complete and unquestioning faith in the virtues, in the wisdom, in the holy disposition and the goodness of the adult. The child, in these years, says Steiner, has the unconscious longing to experience the world as founded in Goodness. Let each look back to his own first memories and perceive with what unquestioning confidence he received all that came to him or her and the circumstances that surrounded him. If there was ugliness, hypocrisy, even cruelty, the child may suffer but accepts it all as the law of his existence. The child of poor parents does not feel his poverty, nor the rich child his wealth. Everything is for him as God made it. With each momentary breath he drinks in all that surrounds him. The faith of the young child in all that *is*, so that he accepts and imitates all and everything just as it is, is one of the most moving spectacles of life. And what the conscious adult can bring forward to meet this Faith is the deepest mood of religious reverence. Therefore Rudolf Steiner says of the teacher of little children in the Nursery Class that such a teacher must have the inner attitude of a Priest, must bring a sacramental mood into all the details of daily life; outwardly free and joyous, of course, and open and alert for all that comes his way, but inwardly filled with a sense of natural piety towards life, above all before the mystery of all that is taking place in the growing life of the little child before him, a mystery based on no earthly considerations but on the deep, pre-earthly resolves that precede earthly birth. One does not look down to the little child, but one looks up with reverence to the wonder of the growing man.

And now as we pass to the second phase of childhood, from 7 to 14 when education includes actual schooling, we come to something different. We have characterized this phase, too, as one in which the child lives vividly in his natural faculty of Imagination. Imitation in a pronounced form gradually recedes and becomes a quality of soul, a love for Authority. This may at first sight seem to contradict ordinary experience, for children are known to be wilful and disobedient, yet the child of these years does rely, for all his essential needs, on the final authority of the adult and a quickly vacillating parent or teacher can bring havoc into a child's life. On the other hand, that which the child hears and sees he does not receive as mere sense-perception, but he immediately transforms it, by an inner act of Imagination, into a picture and the picture impresses itself upon the soul. He really gazes out of a picture world upon the world of sense. Imaginative teaching quickens and enlivens the blood stream and works healthily upon the breathing system; dull, abstract teaching spreads a kind of torpor through the blood and senses and makes the breathing shallow so that the naturally lively child turns into a rebel, and harsh discipline becomes a necessity – hence the traditional picture of the schoolmaster in black uniform, cane in hand. Moralize to a child of these years and you rouse a mood of oppression, of antipathy, and even of hate – a childish hate that rejects impersonally the sermon which the life-filled organism cannot abide. Cast what you have to say into the form of an imagination and the sympathies are quickly roused, and through the sympathies the feelings, thereby alone making a deep impression. That which, as heavenly nature, built up the body in the first seven years must now acquire a life of feeling perception for the world; through the senses of the child, pure spirituality encounters a world of matter, and this, in its essence, is an artistic experience of life, filled not with ideas but with imaginations.

What is 'good and evil' for a small child of 7? There is one brother carrying cake and wine and he meets a little old man, and the little old man is hungry; this brother turns his head away in scorn and passes by but he very soon falls into some trap. There is another brother who has only a crust of bread and a flask of water, but he greets the little old man kindly and shares what he has, and through his deed he acquires a gift for life whereby he may even rescue his proud and greedy brother. How often does this theme occur in one form or another in the fairy tales! And how filled with truth it is, and real for life! To the prosaic mind it may appear that the good are not so easily rewarded, nor the wicked so easily punished, but the child, in his true child nature, is never prosaic. Fundamentally we know that the force of egotism must lead to ultimate imprisonment of soul, but that the heart free from egotism opens a way into the future.

As we advance from 7 to 14 the type of picture changes; at 13 or 14 it may be a human situation, yet it is the situation that speaks to the child and not the abstract logic. The Force of Imagination quickens the powers of sympathy and attentiveness, so that the adult in later years learns to differentiate below the level of the senses, redeeming life from a mere living in a clay prison. We are surrounded today by egotism in every form, but through it all there runs the golden thread of redemption. In the end, for the productive truths of life, the poetic eye sees further than the most exhaustive analysis of scientific facts. Only the artist in man can perceive the forces of destiny that permeate the otherwise dreary facts of existence. These middle years of childhood are the years when the world speaks first and foremost to the heart – when the natural artistry of the child, present as a form of experience in every child, perceives the world as a magical web of destiny unrolling in endless pictures. We stand within the temple of Life and the Gods beckon to us in every flickering light, in every sound and passing form. The earth is not bound and fettered by laws of gravity; the heaven is free, and the flowers rejoice in the sunlight, and the ripening corn is God's bread and the sparkling stream His wine. During these years the artist in the teacher must meet the natural artist in the child – only so can there be true communion between adult and child, even as the Archangel Raphael accompanies young Tobias on his journey, transforming all things into powerful spiritual events that bring healing to the otherwise blind and weary world. So does the eternal child in man restore the Light of the World to the old man grown blind.

Art, then, in the widest sense, is the very ground for the educational work of these middle years. Art is the training whereby the incarnating spirit of man can unite harmoniously with the hard material facts of existence. In his deeper nature, says Steiner, the child in these years longs to experience the world as Beautiful. To experience this in man and nature brings joy into existence, for a theory once thought grows old but an artistic experience must be grasped afresh each time. At the same time to lead the children into regular artistic activities such as painting, modelling, drawing, wood-carving, handiwork, music and eurythmy fortifies the will and strengthens the soul for the arduous tasks to come. This is no sentimental theory but is based on the real facts of human evolution.

What, then, is left for the later years of childhood, from 14 to 18? Now, as we have shown, the element of individual and original thought begins to make its appearance, and for the thinking life of man the world seeks to find its revelation in Truth. But how can we arrive at Truth if knowledge is to be severed from all knowing about the Highest? Does not the

striving spirit of man stand in contradiction to the mere order
of physical creation? Man does not wish to look to an ultimate
Truth as something beyond his reach; he wishes to experience it
directly in daily life. The ordinary knowledge of today leaves man
pining in a cold and comfortless cell; it opens no windows for the
soul but leaves him staring into a physical void; it leads each one
into his own peculiar loneliness.

If, however, the way has been prepared in the previous years,
it is possible to come to real and significant conclusions. All are
agreed today that true observation is a first principle in seeking
for true knowledge, but it is not so commonly recognized that
our faculty of observation is limited by our outlook. If we have
a preconceived notion of a man we see him only through our
notions and not as he really is, and this is true of all knowledge.
It is possible to observe man so that we think of him only as a
higher animal; in actual fact it is because we think of him as a
higher animal that we perceive him as such. But if we observe him
without preconceived notions, then, both in regard to his physical
form which is quite exceptional and in his productive spiritual
nature revealed through the ages, it becomes impossible to derive
his being from the animal kingdom. After all, nature, particularly
living nature, is quite incomprehensible to the modern mind,
and it will continue to be so until men learn to seek its origin
and meaning in higher worlds. Man, however, bears something
of these higher worlds within him and therefore he alone is
capable of evolving a connected inner life; he alone can think
and can conceive a path to freedom; he alone is concerned with
the problem of freedom.

Science, in the sense of a search for Truth, and Truth as an
Ideal, belong rightly to the post-puberty years of childhood.
Here the teacher must be first and foremost a scientist in that
he practises exact and unbiased observation and formulates his
thoughts according to the facts observed. Theories change but
the facts are there and the world is built on them. To work out
of abstract theories upon child nature is to limit personality. To
work in accordance with the needs of child nature – permeating
the first years with the quality of veneration, the middle years

with rich imaginative experience, and the later years with an ardent search for Truth – is to release the very forces that flow as creative power into the thinking of the adult. Then thinking is no longer static, falling into formulas, but is able to accompany the dynamic forces in man and in nature with inner comprehension. Then into the thinking there flow the powers that have built the body and the winged vision of the soul. We think not only as head-men, but with the full force of manhood, and that is no easy matter. The head thinks idly *about* things but man must perceive the world in thought, that is in spiritual cognizance. The Priest, the Artist, and the Scientist stand united in the individual man in each act of observing life: they are not separate but one. We are not concerned with dogma, with aesthetics, with speculative ideas, but with Truth as a primal force of existence shining out in individual human consciousness. Steiner says of adolescents that they have the longing to discover that the world is founded on Truth. Thus education in these years is concerned primarily with a training in thought. *Knowledge is not intended to load the mind but to nourish and to stimulate the activity of thought.*

Religion, art, and science, apart from their treatment as subjects in the school curriculum, accompany the years of childhood as a natural basis for life, unfolding the one from the other, in the life of will, of feeling and of thought, in the three-fold search of man for Goodness, Beauty, and Truth.

Feeling in the Growing Child

We have come to regard feelings as subjective and therefore untrustworthy. We fight shy of them in public and are not a little ashamed of them in private. There have been parents who, in a bout of confidence, have asked uneasily whether our education does not encourage too much feeling for a world as hard and competitive as our own. The fact is that most people have more feeling than they know what to do with; they get distressed about little things and worry about nothings. Feeling is too often confused with emotionalism. A man of strong, rich, deep feeling is a character; an emotional man is a type of horror. It is probably true to say that there is too much emotionalism in our day and too little real feeling. That is why psychology is such a thriving profession. Yet feeling is an essential part of human nature: a man who lacks feeling is hardly human.

Compared with thought, feeling is certainly subjective. A given thought is the same whoever thinks it, just as a given object is the same whoever beholds it. This does not apply to feeling. Even if we communicate our feelings to others, each must still feel in his own way: we can know exactly what another person thinks, we can see exactly what another person does, but we can only sense approximately how the same person feels. Whether we like it or not, we stand in a feeling relationship with everything around us; even indifference is a state of feeling. We feel situations, events, people, ideas, all day long, and these feelings at least colour, if they do not actually form, our judgements. When someone concludes an argument by saying 'That is how I think about it', as likely as not he means 'That is how I feel about it'. Because feelings are so deeply rooted in the personal, we want to be wary of them; on the other hand, to eliminate feeling from our conduct

40

of life leads to disaster. We have seen too much suppression of human happiness and of life itself for the sake of a theory, an abstract ideology.

There is no denying the fact that feelings have to be reckoned with, and that they do not take care of themselves. If we are not to override our feelings or be overridden by them, we need to know them, understand them and, above all, educate them. To deny feeling is to lapse into the inhuman; wherever this has been attempted it has, sooner or later, roused demons of passion of the direst kind if it has not slain the will to live. Only by educating the feeling can we hope to rise above the personal to something nearer the all-human. To feel deeply may indeed mean to suffer more, but it also means to know more, to understand more, to joy more and triumph more greatly – to be more of a man.

The greatest educator of feeling is undoubtedly art. Since art is inevitably bound up with feeling it, too, is largely discredited today as being subjective. Art may *please* us, so it is argued, but it has no value in the struggle for existence. Therefore it is little more than a plaything. To spend time on art, except as a recreation, is so much waste of time. This word 'recreation' is an example of how the mighty are fallen: what can be more wonderful than to re-create the human being – but that is no longer what the word means.

I have watched men and women, however, being re-created by means of art and the allied crafts. During my stay in America I had the good fortune to visit a place called Letchworth Village with over 4,000 'retarded' patients of all ages. Men and women of 50, 60 and 70 years old were still called 'boys and girls'. I have seen these 'boys and girls', mental age described as 2 to 3 years old, doing astonishing things, making lace, tapestry, rugs, a great variety of articles that would do credit to any shop window. Under the guidance of a trained and sympathetic teacher their poor limbs could do what clever heads could not. By means of their work these unhappy debris of modern times were reintegrated into society, were made part of the general community of man.

Shortly following this visit I had occasion to meet a 'top figure' in American education. I pointed out that here was a case not of art as pastime, not of art for art's sake, but art for man's sake. If so much could be done through art and crafts for the mentally sick, lame and blind, what might not be done, by the samemeans,tore-createwhilewithinamentallysickagewhereabstract minds were running ahead of human hearts to the undoing of man: is not this whole age nervously over-wrought and crippled thereby? For every single thing of beauty produced today, there are ten thousand or ten million clever devices, articles for use or decor, mostly ugly, that have a function but which leave the soul hungry and bare. He agreed that art so described could do much if universally applied in schools, not as an extra but as an essential part of everyday education. In fact, he came to life himself in the course of the conversation, left the discreet official behind him and came forward, a warm-hearted man.

Art calls for skill, form and style. Its practice educates right feeling and right judgement. It can even make use of science, if need be, to achieve its ends. All great art is rooted in morality. It is the greatest possible fallacy to suppose that our moral perceptions are one whit less real than our physical perceptions. Quite the contrary! If we hold only to our physical perceptions, we become no more than ph sical perceptions to ourselves, things in a world of things. That is precisely the danger we are in today; man is becoming more and more an object for outer observation and experiment, to be tested, classified and put in his assigned place. If, however, we open ourselves to our moral perceptions and unite ourselves with them, ideals cease to be empty phrases, and we grow to something more than we were. The visible man then appears as a more or less imperfect image of his own higher nature which calls to him incessantly all through life to advance. True art has its source in invisible manhood – in that which makes man by his very nature more than a thing or a conditioned animal. To educate through art is to awaken man to his nobler attributes, to quicken his faculties for a higher perception of the world he lives in, so that he may come to know himself as the being who gives *meaning* to creation. As the world is going at present, man is in danger of falling into a permanent state of coma as regards his true manhood. Unless he can rediscover himself by bringing moral perception into his scientific outlook, unless he can *re-create* himself through an orderly education of heart as well as head, unless his limbs can be guided to serve spirit as well as matter, he may cease to be man and become the prototype of his own misconception of himself, a beast without a mission. Man cannot live by things alone or, for that matter, by bread alone, even if he can, today, turn stones into a kind of bread.

What is it that constitutes the *wholeness* of an organism, making the whole more than the sum-total of its parts? What is that something more? This is one of the questions often asked today by the more progressive spirits of modern science. The same question may be asked of a work of art. A Greek temple or a Gothic cathedral is more than a pile of masonry organized for a specific purpose. What is that something more that includes the stones but is not a product of the stone? Art, like life, makes for *wholeness* of experience, leading from the sensible to the supersensible. That is what promoted Goethe, contemplating the ancient works of art in Italy, to say: 'This is Necessity, this is God'. He felt that the divine-creative forces in Nature find a further expression through the creative art of man. That is why, also, practice of the arts leads man on to self-discovery – makes him something more than he was. Not only is this practice discouraged, but even the appreciation of art is being rapidly destroyed. Economic pressure, social insecurity, doubt and scepticism promote a superficial life of distractions. Radio, television and the cinema contribute daily to a process of human deterioration. Men drown themselves in noise for they dare not be silent – they dare not face themselves. In these circumstances the education of feeling through art becomes a first necessity for the very preservation of health and sanity.

Art makes use of matter to express that which is more than material. Poetry makes use of words to utter what is beyond the articulate. Music calls out in us another kind of hearing, the plastic arts another kind of seeing. Education should be the greatest art of all, calling out a better form of manhood. The teacher co-operates with the unexpressed genius of the child in his care, so that this hidden genius may one day speak his own language, reveal his own powers for life. In a Rudolf Steiner School all practice of the specific arts serves this all-inclusive art of education itself.

With the child of pre-school age we shall not deal here. The little child, as is well known, lives primarily by imitation. For him it is the art of living, of thinking, feeling and doing of the adult that is all-determining. The little child builds up his life upon example; he is receptive to all things, moods of soul as well as sounds and colours. We educate him by what we are; to educate better, we have to *become* better, to grow ourselves.

Education through actual class teaching begins in the first class. From then on, in our schools, the main lesson becomes the outstanding example of an artistic method of teaching. There is nothing set. What comes about each day in the course of weeks, months and years is a free creative act, according to the gifts and endeavours of the teacher in relation to the needs, capacities and conditions of his children. Experiences *grow* from phase to phase, the ultimate goal of each year being *to give birth to a picture of man*. The ultimate goal of the whole education is that human beings shall be so helped and guided in childhood that they may, in the course of their own lives as adults, arrive at the truest possible picture of man. Description, characterization by every means possible, but never definition and clipped conclusion! There is a time for listening and learning, a time for moving, clapping, reciting, practising, conversing, a time for self-expressive individual doing, not according to the clock but as human need directs. What has been thought needs to be felt, what has been felt needs to be willed and expressed for the co-ordination of the whole human being. With the young child, the *picture* given contains the idea, for a picture can always be *felt*; young children experience the world in pictures – they *feel* the world around them long before they think about it. With the older child, especially after puberty, the idea presented needs to resolve itself into pictures drawn from life so that thinking may enter into social living and become a part of it rather than remain a commentary on the outside.

Just as art selects its material with the greatest care for each particular task, so must education – above all in the matter of the main lesson. There is nothing arbitrary about this, for the child is ever the guide. The example often quoted because it is particularly striking is that of the ninth year. We learn to recognize that with every 'forming process' in child development there is a corresponding 'awakening process'. Round about the ninth year the speech centre is formed and the final relationship between lung and heart, breath and blood, is established. There follows a gentle accentuation of the feeling of *self*: for the first time the child becomes inwardly aware that it is alone in the world. This expresses itself variously in different children: in some it leads to assertiveness, in others to a measure of fearfulness. Something must go out from the understanding adult to meet the child.

The curriculum answers the situation in its own way. For example, Rudolf Steiner recommended for the main lesson stories from the Old Testament. These show by example the force of growing personality, the sense of purpose, of struggle and fulfilment, types of behaviour and conduct, what is faithful or unfaithful, steadfast or inconsequent, courageous or cowardly – in all cases how man is intended to be the representative of something higher than himself. A companion period on farming shows how man lives in relation to sun and moon and the seasons: to the earth beneath him, to the plants that grow and the creatures of the field. The farmer and his wife and the whole community of the farm form a picture of the wise coordinating powers of man carrying purpose to expression in outer life. All the other periods of the year combine in the same way to meet what arises as new experience in the child at this time. Thus, during this year, there is given the first important period on grammar, 'the backbone of language', so that with the forming of the speech centre there may also be the beginning of a more conscious use of words.

This is but one example of many that could be given, to illustrate the fact that education is an art to meet the growing process of childhood, and not a thought-out system based on external considerations. The lessons should answer the unspoken questions in the soul of the child, leading him to health, to harmony, to a growing sense of security in himself.

A further example that is particularly striking concerns the child at the approach to adolescence. Up to the age of 14 the child is associated with one class teacher for all main lesson subjects. Now, with the birth of a feeling of greater independence, he enters the Upper School and there confronts a whole number of specialist teachers for the different subjects. He is no longer guided by one particular person, but is left to choose his guide from among the many. Since the child feels differently with regard to himself he enters also into a different environment within the life of the school. Once again outer circumstance meets inner need in a precise way.

Here, too, the subjects are selected to meet the given situation. The child at this stage learns about the struggle for religious independence, about the birth of industry and the shaping of new social and economic conditions, about the rise of democracy and the search for the rights of man. He learns about the structure of the earth, about the structure of the human form, and also the structure of the first great power machines. In the History of Art period he can follow the growth and extension of the feeling of conscious human independence from Egypt through Greece and the Middle Ages into modern times. Something real in the classroom meets a real moment of development in the child. The teacher is not bound as regards his material but relates his knowledge of the subject to his knowledge of childhood; he works out of the powers of his own imagination and with his own sense of fitness so that the growing child before him may learn to discover himself and to feel what it is to be an expressive and creative human being on this earth. Each teacher that confronts him stands before him as a witness in his own degree for the great ideals of manhood. The child is left to coordinate these different testimonies, and this he does first through his feelings and then gradually in his thinking.

It must be admitted that the man of today knows all too little about the nature and origin of the human faculties which he employs all day long. In Rudolf Steiner's conception of man, willing, feeling and thinking are inwardly related so that the one is born out of the other. The little child first walks, then speaks, then thinks, and this sequence can be followed in great detail throughout childhood. Thus, the child up to the change of teeth may be guided more through action, then from the change of teeth to puberty through picture and description and artistic presentation by way of the word, and finally, in adolescence, through a right entry into the realm of ideas. The child *grows into a thinking being* and the education accompanies him in this growth. Then thought lights up in man as a power of inner illumination bringing revelation to the world around him. Man feels himself standing within life and carrying it forward rather than standing apart from it and building abstract theories about it. In this way thought itself becomes creative activity. We gain insight into that which Keats divined when he wrote:

'Truth is beauty, beauty Truth.'

Into this general artistic method of education which adapts itself year by year in the way described and which enters into the treatment of every subject (into the teaching of languages, for example, which enables the child to sense, feel and appreciate the psychologies of folk other than his own) there comes the art work itself. Art includes recitation and drama, painting, modelling, carving, eurythmy and gymnastics, handicrafts of many kinds and other such activities. In all this work it is *the type of exercise* that is all-important and the time when it is introduced. If art is over-directed it becomes mere technique. If, on the other hand, there is unlimited freedom, it becomes a matter of mere self-indulgence. Both ways the true impulse of art is defeated. Art is an extended language and needs its own form of grammar, syntax and the like. Only when these are acquired has the individual the right means for expression so that at the highest level self-expression ceases to be subjective and becomes expression for the whole world. The training through art in a school is not for the purpose of producing artists as specialists, but in order to educate young human beings for the art of living. Art, as already shown, co-ordinates thought and feeling and will so that right judgement may be formed. The best that is in man reveals itself when he can hold his powers in inner balance; then art is not exotic but becomes an utterance of the Word. Every human life truly lived is such an utterance. The greatest and most liberating art is based on sober and disciplined exercise and this is equally true of great living.

The following example taken from work with 6-year-olds will illustrate what is meant by exercise. The children were told a story about a star. Some days later, on their painting morning, they were to *paint* a star. A star shines, it rays out brightly – what is more fitting than bright radiant yellow for a bright shining star? So the children dipped their large square brushes into the liquid paint and formed a bright yellow centre on their slightly moistened paper. The yellow spread easily into a circle. And now, with the same big brushes, the children, beginning at the centre, painted the rays outwards, the yellow growing fainter as it moved further away from its source. Now, in the middle of the paper, there was this great shining star of spreading rays. But there must be something to *hold* the star there on the white paper, even as the night holds the stars in the deep blue heavens. The brushes, having been carefully washed clean, were now dipped into liquid blue and the children began to bring this blue, as if from the furthest heavens, to the edges of the paper. There around the edges the blue was darkest, and now, very carefully, with their large square brushes, the hands of these little 6-year-olds guided the streams of blue towards the star – led the blue, growing fainter and fainter, in between the golden rays, till blue touches yellow on the way to the heart of the golden star. How very carefully they had to guide the blue so that the yellow should remain clean without smudging and so that there should be no dry bare white patches left between. At length it was done and there was the star shining outwards in its yellow and the blue holding it firmly but gently in its place. Half-way through this exercise, as the blue was approaching the yellow but had not yet arrived, one of the 6-year-olds was heard to say in wonder, 'Look, the star is beginning to shine!' It was indeed true – as the blue came inwards covering the white paper the yellow shone outwards ever brighter.

In the exercise there was care, precision, the difficult manipulation of a large brush, cleanliness, appreciation of the qualities of the colours used and, the most important, a *discovery* for the child to make!

This elementary example taken from the very young is true of the entire work which must include at each level the appropriate elements of training, control, true use of material, suitable selection of the task, and room for discovery. Such exercises then flow little by little into 'free expression' so that at the end there is *order in freedom* – and this latter is precisely what the world lacks today. Nor will there be *order in freedom* till there is right judgement, a balance between the directing force of thought and the impelling force of will, which can come only through sound, disciplined feeling.

As mentioned before, one of the most decisive periods of childhood is the transition to adolescence. At this time there is a sudden lighting up in the thinking accompanied by a definite descent into bodily function. The one gives rise to a new feeling of independence and the other to sex maturity. The result is a considerable tension of soul. There are authorities on delinquency who state that a great many recurring criminals begin their unhappy career at this time. In the normal child the mind is open for ideas and ideals whilst there can be, at the same time, a great feeling of loneliness and depression and a longing for understanding companionship. If the education is intellectual and abstract, leaving the life of feeling to its own resources, there can be much chaos of soul: feeling and will are flung back on themselves and give rise to introspection as well as to erotic impulses. The sex creed of today is the outcome of abstract thinking and unbalanced feeling. The true mood of adolescence is to reach out to the whole of life with understanding and love. The primary impulse is one of love for all creation. If, however, the world is presented as a material process only, this impulse of the soul is largely defeated and is flung back on to itself. There are countless people today who intellectually reject the idea of a spiritual ground for existence while subconsciously they long for it, and the result is that their lives are a torment of unfulfillment. An education that guides childhood step by step, carrying will and feeling up into thinking, releases powers of soul for overcoming the feeling of imprisoned impotence that results from unreal thinking and unreal living. Will and feeling flower into imaginative thinking, into insight into the goals of life, into courage and initiative. As a practical measure the art teaching brings to the children the experience of working with the dramatic medium of black and white, the contrast of light and darkness. The conflict that arises in the soul through the longing for the ideal and the sense of being body-bound finds relief in self-expression and a right self-knowledge. Art becomes the mediator and protector, the friend and healer in these difficult years.

Feeling will always be subjective but the subject may grow so that through his feelings he comes into a deeper and more direct relationship with the world of his origin and the goal of his future. When feeling bears the balance of artistic perception, it frees a man from himself, for then he may relate idea to impulse, thought to will, undriven and uncompelled and unswayed by aught but the voice of his own heart. Such a one will also seek the hearts of his fellowmen. This will be the true strength which works through gentleness.

We live in an age when there is, on the one hand, too much direction – making for unfreedom – and, on the other hand, too much abandonment to senseless striving and living, licentiousness masquerading as freedom. It is the middle factor, the balancing factor, that threatens to be eliminated, the life of soul mediating between thoughts and action, between spirit and body. The time has come for the 'pale cast of thought' to be permeated with the warm life-blood of the human heart so that there may arise a new perceiving, a new understanding and a new caring for man and the world. Science itself is coming to this point of view and is awaiting a qualitative change in human thinking. The mathematical thought of the past has produced the machine, largely at the expense of the human heart. The machine is only at the beginning of its possibilities which are great in themselves, but men need new hearts if they are not to be overwhelmed and crushed by the force of their own inventions – and these new hearts can only be born by way of educating qualities of soul, of feeling and of will which can deepen thinking and lead the mind to behold horizons of the spirit.

The Death of Baldur and the Festival of Resurrection

If we would perceive and understand the secrets of human culture in the different regions and peoples of the world, let us awaken once more the feeling of reverence for all that lies concealed in the different mythologies handed down to us from the distant past. The great imaginative pictures of myth and legend are anterior in their origin to the records of history and tell us of a time when human consciousness was not of the intellectual character of our day, but was of a pictorial, dreamlike nature.

That is why children, with their simpler condition of soul as yet free from the intellectual scepticism of later years, take such endless delight in these stories – so that many, if they are not given them by their teachers and parents, seek them out for themselves. That, too, is why, in our Rudolf Steiner Schools, before we come to the study of history as such, we bring to the children these treasures of the past. They are the natural preparation for an understanding of history, if by that we mean an understanding of human destiny and of divine purpose in human life.

We have, preserved to this day, a body of Anglo-Saxon poetry. The earliest Anglo-Saxon work of any completeness is the pre-Christian epic, *Beowulf*. *Beowulf* contains reference to the great hero, Sigurd. Through Beowulf and Sigurd we are led back to all that lived as the great heroic imaginations of the Teuton peoples, in particular to the Sagas of the North, to Odin, Frigga, Thor, Baldur, and the many other mythological figures, the bearers of the great vivifying forces of the people of the north and west of Europe. In this article we will follow up only one

51

thread of this magnificent pre-Christian culture, and we shall try
to see how Christianity comes as the great answer to the mighty
riddles already contained in the human heart at that time.

The Home of Baldur

Odin is the foremost figure of the Northern deities. He is the
Father of the Gods, the All-Father – the great initiator of Northern
culture. Out of the misty conditions of pre-earthly creation, he
emerges as a glorious figure of light. Between the Giants of the
Frost and the Bearers of Fire, the great battling forces of elemental
nature, the powers that condense and the powers that dissolve, he
appears as a being endowed with conscious wisdom – a being of
a higher world.

He separates these warring elements, brings balance between
them, assigns to each its place in Nature, and so creates a
harmony within the tension – and within this new state of
balance is fashioned the world, the stage and seat of human
evolution.

Odin dwelt with the other gods in Asgard, the city of the gods.
With him, too, was Baldur, his dearest and loveliest of sons; for
what was Baldur but the diffused blessedness of heaven's light
through all Nature? In him, Nature found peace, and power to live
and grow. Like a distilled balsam working through all the world,
penetrating all things, he poured his gentle radiance into the eyes
of men, so that their hearts, too, found peace and joy in doing.
Through him, men felt themselves at one with Nature. Their
eyes were 'open'. They were natural-born 'seers' into Nature's
secret kingdoms. We have an echo of this today in the stories
and legends of people, often simple peasants, reputed to have had
'second sight'.

In Asgard, too, was Valhalla, the Hall of the Valiant, of the
Chosen. There Odin himself welcomed the heroes of men, the
champions of earth; they were his fosterlings and especial care.

Often and often did Odin descend from Asgard to Midgard,
the home of men. The way he took was the way of the rainbow,
that most wonderful of bridges that is at once of the earth and

unearthly, the most striking, yet the most ephemeral, symbol of the sky. In many legends and traditions is the rainbow regarded as the bridge between heaven and earth, a bridge upon which the souls of the mighty could walk, and by means of which the gods (the Old Testament would speak of angels) came down to men. As with the rainbow in outer nature, so was thought – the power of thought in man – to be the bridge uniting heaven's mysteries with those of earth.

By way of the rainbow, Odin and the other gods around him paid frequent visits to the earth. There, in human form, they appeared before men. Men gathered round them, seeing them as inspired teachers.

In earlier conditions on earth it was held no miracle that beings exalted above men could appear in human form on earth; nay, this was everywhere expected. In the East such traditions have always existed, leading to the holiest event of all, the Baptism in the Jordan, and the descent of Christ. So, stage by stage were men guided; so were laws and customs founded, and the great religious rites. At appointed times heavenly teachers were born to men – if not heaven's own ministers (the divine principles themselves) whose visits were much rarer, then the chosen of God amongst the human race – the Norse would say, the warriors of Valhalla.

In Asgard then, the Sun city, was the abode of Baldur, the spirit of heaven's radiance.

Odin's Journey

Above Valhalla was Air Throne, the highest seat in heaven reserved for Odin alone. From there Odin could survey the world to its furthest reaches. All things present, great and small, were alike visible to him, and he alone was master of this united knowledge.

There below him was the earth, bathed in ethereal loveliness – not the limited earth of the physical eye, but the earth of springing life and sorrowing decay; the earth of motives, gentle and holy, coming up from hidden sources of the soul to spread in waves and ripples over the wide fields of human endeavour, and the earth of sudden passions clashing like angry thunders, gathering to tempests of threatening destruction; the earth secret as well as the earth manifest – the earth as a dream becoming, in which dream were mingled all the majesty and all the terror of innumerable hosts invisible.

Yet, with it all, his vision was held by things *present*; past and future were concealed from him. A deeper night enclosed even his great light of day. He gazed into creation's womb. The pageantry of countless forms of living and of dying was spread before him, yet the primal purposes and the ultimate ends that might give meaning to the whole were withheld from him. He was himself, in all his greatness, but the child of greater Gods before whose awful grandeur his wisdom waned as thought that sinks unconscious into the oblivion of sleep.

There was one Mimir, a giant, guardian of the Sacred Well of Wisdom. Its mystic waters lit up his mighty figure where he lived on the edge of strange forests and of Odin's darkness. He was the watchman of the Gods at the portal of the higher worlds. Out of those worlds wisdom so echoed in his being that none dared approach him. To him Odin went demanding a drink of the Sacred Waters.

Not for the asking may we receive such gifts. We, too, must give, and freely. We must pluck from ourselves the best of our lesser selves, yield a lesser crown, if we would achieve a greater glory. The Gods do not withhold from us what we have a right to ask, but we must win that right by way of willing sacrifice.

Odin, the clear seer of day, must give one of his two eyes for that which he asked. This he did, but in the moment that he drank the draught, a hidden fount of vision sprang up within him, a hidden music burst upon his listening soul. Through his act he was raised into a higher sphere of life: darkened to the day, he became a seer of the night.

He now saw not only the world present, but the world of origins and fulfilments. Yet now, for the first time, deep tragedy filled his soul; he saw the rising of a tide of evils – he saw the end of all his world. His son, beloved Baldur, must die by treachery and ignorance of his own kith and kin. He could already hear the wail of mournful nature at his death. The fiends of Chaos were to be let loose, and he must see the Vision Splendid of his labours fail into the Twilight of the Gods.

Yet, dimly as the faintest dream, he could see further still. He could see, beyond this time of chaos, sacrifice and sorrow – 'a new green earth appear'. Out of the depths, creation would be formed anew, more glorious, more lovely, more perfected than ever. What was lost would be found again, redeemed to a greater splendour.

Transformed by newborn powers, he descended to the home of men. He wandered over the world from end to end planting in the hearts of earth's children the seed of a new knowledge, the knowledge of death and resurrection. He traversed the world; he passed through regions of frost and cold, through regions of silence and of death, to the uttermost abyss – and there, suspended from Yggdrasil, the tree of destiny, he gazed down into the hungry, raging chasm, where lived the hordes of evil and destruction.

Nine days and nine nights he hung over the abyss. Nine days and nine nights he drank into his being the full agony of that evil – he suffered the pain of worlds. After that time, he returned to Asgard – returned with a secret he could share with none. There he greeted Frigga, his wife, and their son Baldur. He gazed at his loveliest of sons, to see the shadow of the sacrifice already upon him.

The Death of Baldur

There came a time when Baldur the bright, the beautiful, Baldur the joy of heaven and the bliss of human hearts, grew overcast and sad. A great weight pressed upon his spirit. He was haunted by shadows. They entered his dreams. They passed into his thoughts. Gradually they took shape as the wasters of life. His visions failed. The beauty he upheld grew thin and wan to his gaze. He heard the knell of death.

Frigga, the queen, saw the change. Odin the watchful knew that the time of sorrow had come. In the nether worlds, in the ghostly regions, a couch was being prepared.

Could Baldur die? Then day must lose its light, and night its peace. Then gloom must fill the heavens, laughter be stilled, and deadly cold creep over the world. Then glory must sink through twilight into night and heroism be dead.

Could Baldur die? Then Asgard must cease, and the hungry demons of the abyss must mount and swallow up creation. Without light and hope and happiness there can be no life.

What was to be done? Frigga sent her swift messengers throughout the kingdoms of the world. Stones and plants and beasts, the metals of the earth, the spirits of the elements, Gods and men must swear that through them no harm shall come. Willingly they swore. Yet there was one little plant that Frigga overlooked, one small, insignificant little plant, the weakest of things, the mistletoe. Creeping upon the life of others, its pale moon-berries know no brightness. It is a stranger parasite serving itself alone. It lives on death and sucks in poison. Not Baldur, the Sun-being, was its God, but Loki the deceiver, the will-twister; Loki the mischievous hater, the spirit of enmity, exulting in destruction.

Like a snake, Loki crept among the other Gods, jealous of all good, loathing the light, hating all beauty. This Loki, with his thin cunning, was the warp on which the fate of the Gods was woven; the dull grey thread that held the tapestry.

Loki was suffered in heaven for his own special gifts. His wily tricks were called for in emergencies. His nature was to analyse, to know each thing for itself. Out of a total wisdom he made the single thoughts. Where the others created unity, he separated the single things and set each against all. When the Gods think, dreams are born to life; such thinking is wisdom's might. Loki's thinking was other. It was cold, ruthless intelligence, torn from the wisdom-world. His thoughts were arrows piercing the face of life. At his touch life shrivelled. He was destined by his nature to destroy, and he could not be other than he was. All feared him, yet he must be suffered. A deep law, greater than the power of the

Gods of Asgard, said that without death there can be no new life – and he was the instrument of death.

Loki knew the stranger mistletoe; it was *his* plant.

On a day the Gods were assembled around Baldur. Frigga wished to show her triumph. In innocent sport they threw stones and darts and arrows, the most dangerous of missiles, at Baldur. All things had sworn and nought could harm him. Asgard rang with the laughter of a common joy. Then came Loki in disguise. He placed a tiny twig of mistletoe into the hands of the blind God Hodur, brother to Baldur. Unwittingly he threw, and Baldur fell.

Then was joy turned to grief. All nature wept and mourned, all save Loki. The wild glee of his own destructive might was upon him. This was his day.

Came the decree from the lower worlds: let there be in all heaven and earth not one God or man or creature that failed to weep at Baldur's death, and Baldur should live again; in other words, let there be a united will in heaven and earth and he might live. But Loki laughed in scorn. His laughter was the final death-blow. Baldur sank from the sight of Gods and men, sank into the hollow glooms beneath the world.

Loki was left triumphing in his single fury. The brightness of the world was gone. Nature grew cold and human hearts dry. The ugly white light of Loki shone blinding into men's eyes. Heaven's visions died for them. The forces of cold intelligence, greed and enmity, the forces of self-love, were henceforth to rule on earth. Men learnt the sorrow of abiding death, despair, and loss of hope.

This is the story of the Twilight of the Gods – the painful dirge of loss that has sounded through the ages – so that we hear its echo clearly even in the nineteenth century and down to our day.

We may ask, looking at the world today, whom do men really serve – the childlike purity, the innocence and bliss of Baldur, or the fierce intelligence, cruel and selfish and life-denying, of Loki?

It is again the story of the Fall, and the consequences of the Fall. Men have striven singly and in numbers against these consequences, but that is not enough. Except a higher force enter human life, there is no help. Death must follow death to the very end.

The Problem of Baldur

In the death of Baldur we have not a physical but a spiritual event. Baldur faded from the outer spheres of nature to sink into the depths; he faded equally from men's seeing souls to make his home in the depths of their unconscious being. Thereby human life was changed. This change we have all experienced, for it is repeated anew in every human life on earth. Every child on the way to manhood experiences the death of Baldur.

No one has given more wonderful expression to this than the poet Wordsworth. He devoted his best powers to the search for an understanding of man, and to this end made his own life the object of his closest study. No poet has dwelt with greater love and longing on the theme of childhood – a longing as of pain at an irreparable loss. As a child he felt himself near the Gods and one with Nature. As an adult he was outcast and alone. The outer forms and manifestations were the same. The same beauty seemed to be there. Yet something he had known was dead. With all the wisdom of his later life, he could not enter nature as of old. Only in his memory could he recall the bliss and joy of an intercourse with life that was now denied him.

All this he brought to wonderful expression in the opening stanzas of his Ode, *Intimations of Immortality from Recollections of Childhood.*

> There was a time when meadow, grove, and stream,
> The earth, and every common sight,
>> To me did seem
>> Apparelled in celestial light,
> The glory and the freshness of a dream.
> It is not now as it hath been of yore;—
>> Turn whereso'er I may,
>> By night or day,
> The things which I have seen I now can see no more.

A little later in the same poem come the following immortal lines:

> Our birth is but a sleep and a forgetting:
> The Soul that rises with us, our life's Star,
>   Hath had elsewhere its setting,
>   And cometh from afar:
>   Not in entire forgetfulness,
>   And not in utter nakedness,
> But trailing clouds of glory do we come
>   From God, who is our home:
> Heaven lies about us in our infancy!
> Shades of the prison-house begin to close
>   Upon the growing Boy,
> But He beholds the light, and whence it flows,
>   He sees it in his joy;
> The Youth, who daily farther from the east,
>   Must travel, still is Nature's Priest,
>   And by the vision splendid
>   Is on his way attended;
> At length the Man perceives it die away,
> And fade into the light of common day.

In this vision of his childhood's being, Wordsworth finds the consolation for his later years, the assurance of his own soul's origin and immortality. The 'vision splendid' has faded from our sight. Bereft of Heaven's glory, we wander through the noisy years of life; but within the silence of our own souls, in the secluded, personal, and intimate life of memory, we have assurance of the Ancient Glory – it lives in us as a hope and seed for the future. We are not completely abandoned. As children we had not yet reached the powers of the intellect, the powers whereby we can form the Thought of Freedom. As adults possessing these powers, we have grown blind to the super-personal, universal majesty that bathes the innocent dreaming life of children. This is to suffer in ourselves the death of Baldur. The world of intellectual thought that we have entered is a grey, shadowy world compared with the heaven-lit world of childhood.

Such a story as that of Baldur carries blessing to children especially in their tenth and eleventh years. That is a time when they enter on the first trials of dawning self-consciousness and separation. It is as though the angels were leaving go of their hands and they were being told to become men and women on earth. It is as though Baldur himself were speaking to them through this story – as though he were telling them:

> 'Do not be sad and despondent that you must now begin to enter on the hard roads of life. What you are experiencing has to be experienced by all men. It is the way of the world that all mankind must go. In you I repeat my descent into Hell, the place of unrelieved glooms and shadows. But remember the promise of Father Odin, the promise of "a new green earth". That promise lives in you too, and it will carry you forward through the difficult times to come.'

Previous articles (i.e. in *Child and Man*) have been written giving indications of a course of study suitable for older children. We followed the way from the old Sagas with their God-seeing wisdom, through the many changes in human consciousness and their expression in literature down to the nineteenth century. We stopped with the Romantics. We described the mighty visions and aspirations that filled the noblest hearts at that time; how men felt then an accession of new powers to achieve the spiritual, with what great hope they hailed the dawn of a new era. There was to be a gathering of free spirits on earth. The voice of mankind was to sound through the vaults of heaven with a song of new discovery and praise.

But alas, the rattle of machinery was to drown that voice. That rattle was to grow louder and louder and the roar of the engine was to smother all else. The new hopes of freedom, peace, and culture, of the unfolding of human possibilities and the emergence of the divinity in man were all too soon to be overshadowed by the insistent demands, hard and unyielding as the metals themselves, of a new industrial and economic life. Materialism was to raise its banner and all life be plunged into a battle for

earthly prosperity. The joyous announcements of the earlier part
of the nineteenth century grew fainter and fainter in the ears of
succeeding generations.

As Wordsworth had sought comfort in the memory of his own
childhood, so did many, in the hard years that followed, seek to
grope their way back, in a last hope, to earlier conditions of
human life – they sought to reawaken in themselves the childhood
of the race. Hence came such works as *The Earthly Paradise* by
William Morris, and all the efforts of the pre-Raphaelite school
and others.

In Matthew Arnold we have a poet whose whole mood was
filled with the tragedy of his day.

> Well I know what they feel!
> They gaze, and the evening wind
> Plays on their faces; they gaze—
> Airs from the Eden of youth
> Awake and stir in their souls,
> The past returns—they feel
> What they are, alas! what they were.
> They, not Nature, are changed.
> Well I know what they feel!
> Hush, for tears
> Begin to steal to their eyes!
> Hush, for fruit
> Grows from such sorrow as theirs!
> And they remember,
> With piercing, untold anguish,
> The proud boasting of their youth.
> And they feel how Nature was fair.
> And the mist of delusion,
> And the scales of habit,
> Fall away from their eyes;
> And they see, for a moment,
> Stretching out, like the desert
> In its weary, unprofitable length,
> Their faded, ignoble lives.

While the locks are yet brown on thy head,
While the soul still looks through thine eyes,
While the heart still pours
The mantling blood to thy cheeks,
Sink, O youth, in thy soul!
Yearn to the greatness of Nature,
Rally the good in the depths of thyself!

(From *The Youth of Man*.)

Again and again Matthew Arnold sings the death of the Child in
Man; it is the death of spontaneous joy, of natural imagination,
of the naïve experience of the Godhead in all life. The fumes, the
noise, the hardness of the modern city, are death to the soul; but
worse than all these is the loss of the image of man.

And the calm moonlight seems to say:
Hast thou then still the old unquiet breast,
Which neither deadens into rest,
Nor ever feels the fiery glow
That whirls the spirit from itself away,
But fluctuates to and fro,
Never by passion quite possess'd
And never quite benumb'd by the worlds's sway?—
And I, I know not if to pray
Still to be what I am, or yield and be
Like all the other men I see.

For most men in a brazen prison live,

(From *A Summer Night*.)

Later, in the same poem:

. . . . and between
The lightning-bursts is seen
Only a driving wreck,
And the pale master on his spar-strewn deck

With anguish'd face and flying hair
Grasping the rudder hard,
Still bent to make some port he knows not where,
Still standing for some false, impossible shore.
And sterner comes the roar
Of sea and wind, and through the deepening gloom
Fainter and fainter wreck and helmsman loom,
And he too disappears, and comes no more.

Is there no life, but these alone?
Madman or slave, must man be one?

The pain expressed in these lines is not merely the poet's alone.
Neither is it an accident that amongst his works is a poem entitled
Baldur Dead. It is a theme that lay near his heart. Indeed, *Baldur
Dead* might have been the title of his collective work, so much is
it an elegy on an age that has gone.

Again there comes the question – What is the answer to the
death of Baldur? How are we to emerge from the death struggle
that meets us on every side in our modern life? What is our way to
the future? Where are we to find the forces of resurrection? Where
are they at work?

The Mission of the Grail

Such is the wisdom of life, that within the dying we already
perceive the seed of new life. Without death there can be no
new life.

The child must die into the youth, the youth into the man;
and man must die to his own earthly nature if he is to find his
spiritual nature.

As there are laws in organic life, so there are laws in spiritual
life; and as the laws of organic life give modified results according to the external conditions in which they must manifest, so do
the laws of spiritual life vary in the different historical epochs in
which we seek them. That is why there is one wisdom for the East

and another for the West, one for the Greek Age, and another for
our day – but these different wisdoms find themselves united at
a certain point in a single all-human wisdom – and that single
all-human wisdom appeared on earth in the Being of Christ. As
St. Paul showed again and again, in Him each can find his own
special fulfilment. All that was before Christ must be transformed
by His divine alchemy into the new forces of the future.

Baldur suffered death in the spirit; Christ went further, he
suffered death in the body. Odin contemplated the abyss; Christ
went down into the abyss. He gave Himself that others might live,
that others too might have wherewith to give.

The Christ event on earth took place less than two thousand
years ago. That is not long in the history of the world. A
thousand years later, something quite special was born of that
event – something quite new that came to life in the souls of
men. Single men, here and there, following their separate paths
through life, became aware of a temple hidden from outer sight
within the soul, and the search for that temple became their great
goal. In that temple the single individuals, drawn from all quarters
of the world, became one community, fed from a single source
– the deed of Christ. That hidden temple, never to be found by
selfish seeking, was the Castle of the Grail; the wanderers who
came there were the Knights of the Grail.

It is something of the nature of a minor miracle to read page
after page of Malory's *Morte D'Arthur*, to follow the rapid
movement of knightly events, to seek one's way through a
profusion of details feeling everywhere the heroic struggle of
the light-filled moral forces in man against the darker forces of
sensuality and egotism – to follow this narrative through many,
many pages, and then, to turn a page, and quite suddenly enter
a new world – or rather, the same world transformed; to see the
same figures, doing apparently the same things, but imbued with
quite other motives, stirred by a new spirit.

A spiritual fire sweeps through the pages that follow, not a
destroying fire, but the power of the Holy Ghost that kindles
and awakens. The mysterious vessel of the Holy Grail, the vessel
that contains the sacrificial blood of Christ become, through the

resurrection, living spirit; the substance of healing and renewal for all time; the nourisher of all the unfulfilled promise of the human race – this vessel is everywhere, though rarely seen. Many may know of it, may feel its presence, but only they may *see* it, may feed *knowingly* from it, who can die to all fleshy desires and promptings, who have learnt to love the Christ beyond all else.

Sir Launcelot, a noble figure in Arthurian history, is himself excluded. In a dream he realizes his own unworthiness, how entangled he is still in himself, how much a victim of his hungry senses. Yet his child, Sir Galahad, than whom can be no purer soul on earth, is destined to achieve. He stands before us, from the first a free moral being. The Highest Good is his immediate search. Child of Launcelot, he begins where his father ends. He not only finds the Grail; he is proclaimed King of the Grail: but in that glorious moment, his body falls away from him and he enters into the living Christ. He dies into the Christ.

Such a fate leaves us wondering, until we realize that here is no ordinary mortal scene enacted but a high mystery, a chapter from the spiritual history of man; for mankind as a whole, an event of the distant future, an event that would say to us: Christ *is* in the world. But to know Him we must become one with Him; to become one with Him we must die to our earthly natures.

Through Christ's descent into the innermost sanctuaries of the human soul, the spiritual forces in men can grow to such power that even while dwelling within the body, the spirit of man may know himself as a member of a heavenly kingdom. Man may stand planted in outer life, but his spirit – which is not of this world but of the Father which is in Heaven – that spirit, even as earth-dweller, may find the Castle of the Grail, may be nourished with the forces of transubstantiation, may know the Christ. Through such an experience the outer events of life, whilst remaining apparently the same, are actually transformed. All life acquires a new meaning and a new value. The world of outer life is no longer seen from the aspect of the senses but with the eye of the spirit.

The last part of Malory's *Morte D'Arthur* is remarkable not so much for what it contains as for what is omitted. As suddenly as we entered the magic History of the Grail, so suddenly do we now leave it. We are again at the beginning. The same characters are there. The old narratives are resumed. We read on with a sense of disappointment, for it is as though the Grail had never been mentioned. It is just this feeling of disappointment that is all-significant. We realize the world cannot go on in the old way. Inevitably the heroes die, one after the other, down to the sadly beautiful death of Arthur himself. The old brotherhood that he had ruled so gloriously breaks up. If there is to be a true brotherhood of men again it can only be a brotherhood of the Grail. The book does not say it, but we know in our hearts that it is true.

The story of the Grail is the new Saga for human life, a Christian Saga. In it the old Sagas are transformed through Christ. The old Sagas were sung into the listening hearts of men by Angels and Higher Powers. Men heard them, remembered them through the generations, and transcribed them for later days. The new Saga was first conceived and heard on the Earth itself. It was born directly out of the human soul, and the sound and the glory of it is destined to grow and expand to fill the heavens.

The French and German versions of the Grail differ in many respects from the English. They have another hero, Parsifal. Sir Galahad is so godly a figure that he might represent for us the very end of all human endeavour, when death and mortality shall have been overcome, when the world as it is shall have passed away and only the Word, the Christ and His Kingdom, shall remain. In Parsifal we have a being exalted beyond the common lot of men, yet nearer our time. We understand him better. He is our very selves immersed in the great struggle of human destiny. He walks each step of the way that all must walk if they would come to Truth. To write at full length about him would take us too far and must be reserved for a later article.[1] Here we would only indicate a few essential facts.

We see him as a child united with nature. We see the questioner

---

[1]See Francis Edmunds, *Anthroposophy as a Healing Force* (Rudolf Steiner Press, London (Distributor); 1968), and 'The Trials of Parsifal' in *The Golden Blade 1981* (Rudolf Steiner Press, London; 1981).

slowly awaken in him as it must in all men, and with the questioner the search for an Ideal upon which to shape and model his life. He sees that Ideal in knighthood and achieves all that a good knight may. He wins lands, honour, love, and fame. There seems no more he can do.

Vaguely he wanders forth in search of his mother whom he has not seen since the day he left her, a foolish, untrained boy. He wanders on not knowing that she is dead, and, quite unwittingly, stumbles upon the Grail. In ignorance he enters and witnesses the holy mysteries of suffering man. He sees a sick king, Anfortas, and a multitude of knights. All seem to have been expecting him, to be awaiting something from him, but he is unaware of this. Anfortas even gives him the sword of the Grail, a spiritual sword to wear beside his own. He takes the gift, not knowing its meaning or worth. In ignorance and stupor he goes to sleep.

In the morning the castle is empty. The sword-gift is beside him, but there is not a soul to be seen. Perplexed, he wanders forth. As he leaves the castle the gates close behind him, and in that moment the accuser in his own soul awakens. He hears a voice cry after him 'Fool! Accursed! Outcast!' The castle and grounds disappear behind him; they are not of this earth. Slowly the meaning of the words dawns upon him and with it a feeling of unutterable failure. *He had been called and was found unready.* All that he had hitherto valued becomes worthless to him. Love itself grows bitter for him, earthly fame a mockery. The outer world is still there, the world where he had achieved the bounds of success. Now, facing the newly awakened inner man, he is the poorest of knights, indeed outcast, wretched, and accursed. He has seen the Kingdom, and that Kingdom is now denied him. He is filled with insatiable longing to re-enter the mystic castle, to make good his failure.

Long years follow, years of homeless wandering, of despair, of endless struggles, hopes, and disappointments. Nowhere can he find that which he knows exists. At length he meets a hermit. From him he learns the mystery of man revealed in Christ. Now for the first time a void in his being is filled up. Spiritually renewed and refreshed, he goes forth once more, with undivided mind. He now knows what he then had lacked. At length, at a moment least expected, a messenger from the Grail Castle comes to lead him back there. Now as a man, with all the marks of manhood's sorrows, he re-enters the holy place of his youth's great vision. Now he understands pain and suffering and the only source of healing. As knower in the Spirit he is proclaimed King of the Grail. Through his knowledge the dying Anfortas is restored to health. Parsifal now stands before us as the leader to a new phase of human culture and experience. As a new man, as a new seer, he becomes the representative of our own times. He is the new man in every man, the spiritual man to be born from within our mortal natures.

. . . And Today

In the most wonderful way Rudolf Steiner brings the theme of the Grail and Parsifal into connection with education.

In the eleventh class, with the help of Parsifal, we can meet the great forces of idealism in our youth, their enthusiasm for the future. We need not leave them foundering, bewildered, and discouraged in the face of all that threatens life today, with the heartless picture of a mere struggle for existence. We can awaken in them the feeling for the great spiritual powers that lie imminent in man, powers that will lead him from physical to spiritual conquests. We can show that that which man lives by is not his physical but his moral nature. As we were able formerly to bring before him the old heroes, Sigurd, Beowulf, who follow in the way of Baldur and who, glorious as they are, must each in turn die, so we may now show the birth of the new heroes, Sir Galahad, Parsifal, Lohengrin the son of Parsifal, who follow in the wake of Christ and who will go forward with Him into the future, to the fulfilment of Odin's promise of a 'new green earth' and a new humanity.

We may go further than this. We may take example after example to show how the forces of death are led over into forces of new life.

By what power was Shakespeare able to pass on from his

tragedies, his death-dramas, above all from *Hamlet* – dramas that end in disillusionment, defeat, disappointment, and death – to a play like *The Tempest* that abounds with new vision, with new energies for life; that shows treachery conquered by knowledge and discord by love; that sees emerging out of the old world a 'brave new world?' By what powers is Goethe able to take the old Faust as he appears in earlier versions, including the *Dr Faustus* of Christopher Marlowe, a man doomed to inevitable destruction, and to create out of him a quite new Faust for whom service is love and love is service; to lead him through trial after trial of the soul to the pinnacle of man's awakening to his higher destiny, a destiny in Christ, so that though he may not speak the Word, Christ speaks in him? How does Dostoevsky create out of the untold misery, darkness, decrepitude, and bafflement of man as he knew him, such a figure as Alyosha, in whom we feel a new man born of the old with powers unconquerable in the face of life? By what power is Wagner able to recreate in music the *Twilight of the Gods*, and then to rise to the sublime beauty of *Parsifal*, a work which heralds a new future and shows the ultimate triumph of the immortal spirit of man?

In all these mighty men of later human culture we experience the meeting of old and new, of past with present and future; we experience death and, through death, resurrection.

We may ask, who is the suffering king Anfortas? He is a being who should be the leader of the Grail, the leader of the spiritual culture of mankind – but he cannot lead. He has sunk too far into the life of the senses, has succumbed too far to the forces of dying nature; the world is too strong for him. He lacks the powers necessary to his day if the light of Heaven is to continue to shine clear and calm in the souls of men. Knowing of Christ, he has yet lost him. He must await the coming of a new man – of a new force in man. He awaits Parsifal.

Every human being that grows conscious today grows conscious first of the pain of Anfortas, grows aware of the spiritual heritage of man that he cannot by his own powers sustain. There is a night-time in the life of every heroic soul, for the way of true heroism must ever lead through death. Yet, however sick we may be with the pain of Anfortas, we may yet know the healing that can come through Parsifal. We must be willing to travel his road if we would achieve his end.

During the three Easter days we may experience the full cycle of human evolution, the death of Baldur out of the heavens, the unutterable darkness and gloom, and the ascent of the spirit of man from out of the depths. In Christ, his Crucifixion, burial, and Resurrection, all this is fulfilled. In Baldur we are led from life to death: in Christ, through death to resurrection.

Animal Teaching
in the Fourth Class

Northern Mythology is very important for children aged about
10. The moral imaginative pictures of these stories make a direct
appeal to the feelings of children of this age, and, through the
feelings, to the heroic element of Will. It is our object, in this
article, to show how we may lead children of the same age along
their first steps towards the observation of nature. It will not yet
be a scientific approach in the modern sense. Our task will be to
present Nature to the children in such a way that we may call forth
in them feelings of wonder, sympathy, reverence, enthusiasm; we
wish to bring into play their own powers of fantasy. Such feelings,
experienced in a right relationship to facts, and such activity of
soul will later be transformed, with the growing life of thought,
into a true scientific interest in the world – a warm, searching
interest that will not stop short at cold, surface objectivity, but that
will lead the thoughtful student to enter also into a moral-artistic
relationship with the phenomena of life. Observation reveals the
facts, thought can penetrate to the laws, the artist in man can lead
us to the creative source, and religion unites us with that creative
source: all these together make up a knowledge of life, and we
must pay attention to all these in our lessons.

The mythologies can awaken in the children a feeling for the
moral-creative forces in the soul of man. Now, in looking at the
forms of nature, they can learn to feel that these are life-filled
images of the creative powers of heaven. In the Fourth Class we
consider the kingdom nearest to man, the animal kingdom.

*   *   *   *   *   *   *

How shall we begin our approach to the animals? Our starting-point must be man himself – man who alone in all nature has been raised to a free, upright position. Around man we see how the animals, in successive stages from the apes downwards, fall away from this free, independent uprightness to ever humbler conditions of earth-bound existence. Of the animal it is possible to say that what we perceive of its bodily form and processes marks the limit of all its possible experiences. With man, this can never be the case: the bodily form and processes are, at most, but the groundwork for what is truly human. The most trivial conversation is proof of this. The life of thought, of feeling and of will carry us completely beyond the bodily as such.

We will begin, then, by speaking quite simply about man himself. What follows in inverted commas may be regarded as a summary of lessons given in class.

*   *   *   *   *   *   *

'Look, children! Here is the head. It is like a ball – the roundest part of the human body. How different it is from the long arms and legs, the limbs! They are as different as can be – and between them is the trunk which is different again. So we can see three parts – the head, the trunk, and the limbs.

What do we do with the head? In the head we have eyes with which to see the things around us; we have ears with which to hear; we can smell with the nose; we can taste with the tongue. Without the head the world would be quite dark; no sound could reach us; there would be no scents and odours; there could be no taste.

Last year you learnt about chaos, and how, out of chaos, God created the world. Without the head the world would be chaos for us. With the head we learn about the world. We not only learn but we think about the world, and so we can come to understand all the many things around us. When we think, the light of God shines in us and lights up all things.

The head is the roundest part of the body. And what is the

roundest thing in the world? It is the sun! The sun in the heavens is quite round. The sun lights up all the world. The Head of man is like the sun whose light fills all the world.

The sun does not live only for itself. It hides nothing. It holds nothing back. It sends its light to the moon, to the earth, to all the world. It sends its powers to the earth so that all things may grow. Without the sun nothing could live, could it? All things that live owe their life to the sun.

The head, too, does not live only for itself. It takes in food. It breathes in air. Whatever it takes in, it passes on to the trunk so that the whole body may grow and be strong. What it learns of the world, what it takes in through eyes and ears, what it thinks, it also sends down to the body so that we can act and do things. The more we learn, the more we are able to do. The head helps us to know about the world. Then we can learn to love the world.

The trunk is not round. The head is always the same shape, but the trunk never is. It changes its shape with every breath. It is always changing. What do you know that is always changing its shape, now being fuller and now thinner, always waxing and waning? The moon! The trunk is not round like a ball; it is more like *part* of a ball, like a crescent moon.

In the trunk we have the lungs with which we breathe, and as we breathe in and out the chest rises and falls. So, too, as the moon waxes and wanes the great tides of the earth rise and fall, like a mighty breathing. Mariners must watch the rise and fall of the waters very carefully. They are always looking to the moon. Remember your farmer of last year. Farmers also watch the moon, for they know that the rains come with the moon. The moon helps all things to grow. The trunk too, works for the whole body so that the body may grow.

And now think of the limbs. With our arms we can stretch out in all directions – we can reach out towards the farthest things, towards the stars even. Indeed, when we stretch out our fingers wide our hands are themselves like stars. We can point to the heavens from which we are born. Our feet point to the earth below us that supports us. Heaven and earth have built our limbs.

So, when we look at a man, we can think of sun and

moon and stars, of the whole heavenly world, and of our mother earth.

And now, let us think of the limbs again.

What can you do with your legs and feet? And what can you do with your arms and hands? How much more you can do with the arms and hands! What do you do chiefly with your legs? They carry the trunk from place to place over the earth. They are the bearers of the trunk, and they also belong very much to the earth.

But the arms and hands are quite free from the earth. We can lift them to the heavens, we can fold them in prayer, we can also till the earth, we can write, we can paint and model, we can play music, we can do a thousand things. The legs serve the trunk. With our hands we can serve one another.'

*   *   *   *   *   *   *

It is important for children to be taught in such a way that when they look at a man they may *feel* there is much more than they can see – in man are assembled all the powers of worlds, visible and invisible. His form is not earthly but is born of heaven. What the sun does for plants, lifting them away from the earth, is what the spirit of man does for man, raising him to the free upright position.

After such an introduction, extended over several days and interspersed with much conversation, we can proceed to select characteristic types of animals. The descriptions must be vivid, accurate, dramatic, and filled with contrasts; our aim is to give living characterizations. The children must feel – we enter a magic world. The word 'magic' is connected with the word 'Magi' – with an entry into the deep wisdom of the world, a wisdom that is beyond ordinary sense and reason, that is quite beyond mere logical cause and effect. The various animals are living images of divine thoughts. When men think they have *ideas*. With these ideas they direct their conduct and achieve results in the world. When the Lords of Creation think, they engender *beings*, for so has the world been made and all that is in it. The thoughts of man are reflections of the deeds of Heaven. To man is given a life in ideas because he is himself the central Idea in all the created universe. To speak in terms of the Gospels, he is the expressed image of the living Word – the Word that became flesh. in man alone does the God, 'I AM' find immediate utterance. Looking from man to the kingdoms of nature, we perceive there the dismembered parts of all that in man has been brought to the perfection of harmony. We can perceive in the separate animals a one-sided development of particular parts of man. From a study of the animals alone, including even the higher apes, we could never conceive the form and appearance of man. Looking at the human form it is comparatively easy to recognize the origins of the different animal creations. For such a view we are indebted to Rudolf Steiner. It is a view that does not divorce us from the fruits of scientific observation; on the contrary, it makes full and adequate use of them. It is a view that would teach us to look at nature from above downwards rather than from below upwards. Stage by stage we can descend from the heights and, having grasped the depths, re-ascend to the heights. Merely to build from below upwards is to construct, in modern terms, a Tower of Babel that must surely end in confusion. Man, who stands at the pinnacle of earthly creation, is at once the central edifice and key to the understanding of the creatures around him.

Having formed thoughts about man, we can now turn to the animals. Our first approach will be from the aspect of form – what can the *form* teach us? To this end we have selected certain animal types whose *forms* can be specially suggestive. Rudolf Steiner recommends especially the cuttlefish, the mouse, and the horse.

*   *   *   *   *   *   *

'Children, deep below the surface of the water, far from the air and the light, there lives a creature called a cuttlefish. This creature has a rounded hollow body. The walls of this body are like a shell. One end is closed and round like the back of the head. The other end is like a big, open mouth. With this mouth it takes in food. It also takes in water and so it breathes. The food we take into the mouth we send to our stomach. The air we breathe through our nose we send to the lungs. With the cuttlefish, mouth and stomach, nose and lungs are all one, and all this is inside the head for it has no separate body or trunk. It has two big eyes, one on either side of this head, just behind the mouth. It has no ordinary lips, but its lips are drawn out into six long feelers which are forever moving this way and that. Sometimes they open out wide like the petals of a flower, and other times they draw close together. These drawn-out lips, or feelers, take the place of arms and legs. They help to direct it from place to place. It also has two long suckers. Perhaps these take the place of a tongue. With these it can seize hold of its food and draw it into its hungry mouth. When it is not using its suckers it carries them folded back in little pockets on either side of the mouth.

It also has something else. Do you know what 'Tinte' means in German? It means 'ink'. In German the cuttlefish is called a Tintefisch – an Ink Fish. It has a little pouch reaching up somewhat like a nozzle. When it meets something it does not like, something that makes it afraid, it suddenly spurts out, through this nozzle, a dark inky fluid. The inky fluid spreads out like a dark cloud making a screen which hides it and so it can get away more easily. This is really very clever though I do not suppose the cuttlefish knows that.

Think of the cuttlefish in the water. It has no trunk, no real limbs. It is really just a *head*, and it has made for itself just what a head would need if it had no trunk and limbs to help it. What the cuttlefish does with its feelers and suckers and opening and shutting mouth, we do with our heads when we watch and listen and take in the things we wish to learn. And sometimes I have noticed even this – that when you do not wish to learn something, you do very much what the cuttlefish does when it hides itself behind a cloud of inky fluid. It really does happen sometimes that when I think you are in the class listening to me, with your heads you are very far away and I have to call you back.

Remember this then, the cuttlefish is a *head* animal – it is really all head. It does not *think* as we do. Its life there below the water is like a kind of dream.

Of course, there are many other head animals. (One little boy –
the octopus! Another child – the jellyfish!) Yes, and there are still
other animals that are really head animals. Think of the head. It is
all hard outside. Do you suppose it is hard right through? What
animals are there that are hard outside and soft inside? Do you
know the mussel? It has a shell outside and is soft inside, and it
is always opening and shutting like a mouth. Then there is the
crab, the lobster and others. They are all hard outside and soft
inside like a head; and even the limbs are not at all like our limbs
– they too are hard outside and soft inside as though they have
just grown out of the head body – all such animals are really
head animals. We will speak more about these animals later.'

*   *   *   *   *   *   *

'To-day we will think of the fish – an ordinary fish. It really has
no head to speak of but only a kind of head end to its body with
eyes and a big mouth in it. It has no real limbs but only fins and
a tail. The fish is really all trunk from beginning to end. That is
why it has so many bones, like little straight ribs, running all the
way down its body.

How gracefully the fish can bend its body this way and that.
As it dives and darts and curves in the water, it seems to speak to
us with its trunk. And how hungry this trunk can be sometimes!
With a lash of its tail it leaps forward and just snaps with its head
at anything it sees to eat – just as you might leap forward with
your legs and take hold of something eagerly with your hands
– and then the trunk is quite happy and can remain still for
quite a long time. So the head and the tail and also the fins
are all like special limbs serving the trunk. The fish is really a
trunk animal. It is altogether different from the cuttlefish.'

*   *   *   *   *   *   *

'Now let us think of quite another creature – the mouse. You
have all seen a mouse, I expect. You cannot say the mouse has a
head resting on shoulders. It looks much more as though the trunk

grew on into a head, and this head-part narrows down quite to a point – a very inquisitive little point that is always busily sniffing at everything. And then, just at this point, you know how it has long trembling whiskers growing out on either side; the whole mouse seems to follow what these trembling whiskers tell it; the whiskers know at once when a cat is near. And now, inside the mouth there are sharp pointed little teeth. How busily the mouse works with them, nibbling and nibbling; not only does it nibble at food very, very quickly, but it can nibble a hole or even a tunnel for the whole trunk to go through. A mouse's teeth never stop growing; they must always be kept strong and sharp. It has quite tiny little beady eyes, but very large ears that stand out from its head like sentinels. Altogether the head is a very useful tool for the trunk, or rather a whole set of little tools working together for Master Trunk.

The tail of the mouse is quite special, too. It is long and thin but very strong. It has little rings running down it almost to the very tip, and a mouse can really stand on its tail when it is trying to climb up the side of something.

So what is the mouse really? It has quite a long trunk, and the head is a kind of limb, and the tail is a kind of limb, and then it has its four little legs which carry the trunk along.

The mouse, too, is just a *trunk*, and everything else serves this trunk.'

*   *   *   *   *   *   *

'Think of our friend, the pig – *there* is another famous creature for you. It is really very difficult, isn't it, to know just where the trunk begins to be head. In the pig, too, this trunk-head tapers down, this time to the hard horny snout. What does it do with its head-snout? It is always working away with it, digging and turning up the earth or the rubbish heap, looking for something to eat; how it snorts and grunts as it works; how eagerly it swallows, swallows, all it can to feed its great, big, heavy trunk. Its eyes are quite buried in flesh. Its large ears flap lazily down. The snout is the chief instrument, and the greedy mouth just below it. Its four legs just trot about – pig's trotters – carrying its heavy trunk from place to place; that is all they can do. You can see, in the pig, that what matters is the trunk. The pig also is a *trunk* animal.'

*   *   *   *   *   *   *

'Let us think of the noble horse. What graceful legs it has! How it beats the ground with its hoofs and sends the turf flying when it is impatient to be off! How beautiful it is to watch a horse galloping across a green meadow or along the ridge of a hill! Have you ever sat on a horse at full gallop? It is the nearest thing to flying.

This graceful, certain movement, this lightness and speed, making it the swiftest of creatures, the horse owes to its legs.

And in the cart-horse, how strong and sturdy the legs are!

These wonderful legs all serve the trunk to carry it about. That is their only work. Now watch a horse walking. For example, watch a horse pulling a plough or a cart. Look at the head as it does so. The head moves up and down with every step. The head is not free as in man; it is much more like a part of the trunk made into a head. When it is grazing, with its long neck stretching to the ground, and its strong teeth tearing at the grass, the head of the horse is just like another limb serving the trunk.

Let us think, too, of the humble cousin of the horse – the ass! The ass is certainly not graceful. It does not move easily – as you know, sometimes it refuses to move altogether. Have you ever seen an ass gallop? And if it does move more quickly than usual, it is awkward and bumpety. But now try and go up a stony path on a mountain side. How wonderfully *sure-footed* it is, as it picks its way step by step over boulders and stones. The path may be ever so narrow, and the mountain side very steep, but leave the ass to pick its way and do not hurry and it will prove a very good ass indeed and will bring you quite safely to the end of your journey. So the ass may be obstinate and stupid in some ways, but it is very, very *wise* in its legs.

When the horse neighs it is like a champion calling to his mates, but when the ass brays it is telling a sad, sad story of all the burdens it must bear on its shaggy back and of a road that is always too long.

Wonderful in their different ways as are their legs, the horse and the ass are still trunk animals. It is the trunk that is all-important, and all else serves the trunk.'

*   *   *   *   *   *   *

The above are naturally but sketchy descriptions. In class one can enlarge on all this. The children draw pictures of the animals. It is important to describe the environment characteristic of each animal. One can tell animal stories, can recall fables they know and add less familiar ones from the different peoples of the world.

With reference to the last group of animals, the mammals, different though they may be in shape, size, appearance, habits of life, environment; nevertheless one principle clearly prevails – they are, one and all, essentially trunk animals with head, legs, and tail as particular appendages. There is no real threefold division as in man.

We have spoken to the children of head and trunk animals. The question naturally arises, are there also *limb* animals, i.e. creatures whose essential nature is vested in the limbs? We discover the remarkable fact, emphasized by Rudoflf Steiner, that there are not. This can come to the children as a great wonder, and it leads us back once more to man. As Steiner points out, man is the only being who has *real* limbs – limbs that have a life of their own quite apart from their service to the body. It is the limbs of man that make him truly man. We can compare the human head to the cuttlefish. We can compare the human trunk to other animals, but in all nature, there is nothing to compare to the *human limbs*. There man is unique!

What a miracle are the human hands! Let us think of them, for example as in Dürer's picture, folded in prayer. How much individual life and expression there is there! A whole soul dwells in those hands. Let us think of the hands of a musician – in every movement of the fingers there is a world of expression; the careful, precise hands of a mathematician; the fine, disciplined hands of a surgeon; the skilled hands of a labourer; the hands of an actor that almost speak to us; or just *hands*, any human hands – what wisdom, spirituality, variety is contained in them! How loving they can be, or how cruel! They are indeed not merely tools of the body but something in themselves, real *limbs*, the bearers of the *will* of man, the agents of destiny.

What the hands have gained in freedom, that the legs have sacrificed. They are much more limited in function, much more bound to the earth – yet they, too, show in their uprightness, in the straight line with the knee-cap characteristic only of man, a degree of emancipation from the earthly, from the all-binding force of gravity, possessed by no other creature. The legs, too, in their expressiveness completely transcend their merely functional nature. The walk of a man is quite individual. In their own particular way even the legs are not merely servants of the body but are servants and agents of the spirit.

The human limbs are indeed a wonder of creation, and this all-important fact we can bring home to the children.

We are, after all, at this stage in the education concerned only with broad and fundamental facts. As a seed for their future the children can receive the thought that the animal world finds its meaning only in relation to man; that the animal kingdom finds its synthesis and higher unity in the being of man. Without man, nature would be meaningless. Such a thought is, as yet, but little acknowledged. Yet, without this thought life is lacking in all real purposiveness: we are merely plunged into materialistic utilitarianism and a Darwinistic blind struggle for existence. We must rescue man from a point of view that would deprive him of all dignity, and ultimately of all humanity.

We can remind the children of the story they had the previous year of Adam naming the beasts. He surveys them with a God-like eye; he alone knows them in their innermost nature and he pronounces this knowledge in the name. We can remind them, too, of the Farming period they had; of the farmer, the husbandman, the being who can *care* for all nature around him. These are real pictures of man.

*   *   *   *   *   *   *

It is always valuable in education to describe the same thing to the children from different points of view. This stirs the will and the imagination whereas mere definition cramps and limits them.

Having described such animals to the children, we can – perhaps in the same term but better still a little later – make quite another approach. So far we have dealt principally with the *forms* of man and the animals. We can now take the three contrasted types of animals, the eagle, the lion, and the bull, in relation to the *functions* of head, heart, and limbs in man. The traditions of wisdom have always grouped these together around the being of man. Zarathustra in his first vision of the Sun-Spirit, Ahura Mazda, perceived Him in human form seated on a throne supported by a lion, an eagle and a bull with three hierarchies of Angelic Beings ranged above Him. In the Sphinx we have a human face, the wings of an eagle, the chest of a lion, and the lower trunk of a bull. We are reminded, too, of the Vision of the Apocalypse with the eagle, the lion, the bull and the human form. There is a great truth contained in this symbolism. At the present stage we can discuss these three types quite simply.

*   *   *   *   *   *   *

'Children, let us think now of the King of the Birds, the Eagle. Where does he live? All alone, in high rocky places. His fierce eyes seem to pierce every distance, as, from his eyrie high above, he surveys the world below him. His long, strong beak is like an iron limb of terrible power and strength. When he is not in his stronghold, you see him hovering high in the heavens on wide, outstretched wings. Suddenly he swoops down to the world below; he has seen a lamb, maybe. And now with his iron beak or his strong talons he has gripped the lamb, and with rapid strokes his wings carry him back to his lofty home to consume his prey in solitude.

If we wished to compare the eagle with some part of man,

which part do you think he resembles? See, the head. The shoulders of man are themselves like rocky crags, and on these the head rests, looking out over the world. The head itself does not fly off, of course, but our thoughts do, and we think with our heads. We may seem to be resting but our thoughts can be far away; they can carry us everywhere in an instant. Our thoughts can fly to the heavens, they can descend to the deeps. We can look back in our thoughts to the past and we can look forward to the future. We seize hold of what we see and hear; whatever we take hold of with our thoughts, we make our own. We carry it off, like the eagle, to the lonely fastness where we live in our heads and there we devour it.

How different is the eagle, in its airy heights, from the cuttlefish living below in the dark waters; yet they both remind us of the head we carry on our shoulders.

Think, too, of the shrill, piercing cry of the eagle. I expect you have never heard it. You know that when you make a squeak sound, which some of you are fond of doing sometimes, it seems to come from high up in the head. Perhaps you have been to the Zoo and visited the bird houses. When you hear the very high twittering sounds of some of the little birds, and watch them flying swiftly from perch to perch, they are like a cloud of gaily dressed little thoughts, like a lot of little feathery heads flying about.

The shrill eagle's cry is a *head* cry; compare this sound with the deep soft moo-ing of a cow or with the deep bellow of a bull; these sounds are not at all head sounds – they come from much deeper down.

Now think of cows in a meadow. How they love to rest comfortably on the rich green earth. How quietly and contentedly they chew the grass. Can you imagine a cow taking a flying leap at a tuft of grass and carrying it off at a gallop to a corner of the field to devour it greedily? The cow, with its great, heavy body, is so very different from the eagle – the broad mouth with the thick soft lips, so different from the horny pointed beak! And what do they do, these cows? They change blades of green grass into white flowing milk – and this milk is not at all for themselves, they give it all away. What can the cow teach us as it changes grass into milk that it gives away? It teaches us that what we learn is not just for ourselves; what we learn we shall change into powers to help our fellow-men. We take in what we learn and we change it into ways of working for others. This is not at all easy. You know that a cow has *four* stomachs; you have watched a cow chewing the cud. It does not chew the grass just one, but many, many times. It goes over the same food again and again before it can make it into pure, white milk. So, too, we must go over what we learn again and again – and only in years to come shall we be really ready to use it.

And think of the angry, stormy bull charging across a meadow. He holds his head down like a battering ram and charges forward as though he would move mountains form his path. Where does the might of the bull chiefly live? Is it in the head? No, he uses his head merely as a weapon. The mighty drive of the bull comes from behind where he beats against the earth with his hind legs, hurling himself forward. What can the bull teach us?

Think of man at work. Think of him driving the spade into the earth, turning wild places into fertile fields. Think of him digging rocks and stones out of the mountains to make his great buildings. Think of him seeking out the heavy iron to make his vast engines and machinery. Think of all the many hard things men must do. It is the bull in man that gives him the strength to do all this. In your morning verse you speak of 'the strength of human limbs'. It is the hidden bull in man that gives him this strength.

We can now think of the lion, the King of the Beasts. The roar of the lion certainly does not come from the head; nor is it like the deep bellow of the bull; it comes from his mighty chest, crowned with noble mane and head. With this roar he commands the jungle. We can think of the lion, first crouching very still, all drawn together, and then making a great and sudden spring through the air. He is so strong, the lion – stronger than the huge elephant, and yet he can move so gently and quietly through the grass or jungle that there is not the faintest sound. The eagle carries the lightness of the air; the bull, the heaviness of the earth; the lion comes between. The eagle swoops, the bull charges, the lion leaps – and in his leap through the air he is the most graceful of all animals, for he is, at the same time, light and strong. The crouch and spring of the lion, the drawing together and the leaping forward remind us of the heart we carry in our breasts; the heart of man does this always – that is the beating of the heart that we hear. We carry a lion in our heart; that is why, when a man is very courageous and also gracious and gentle, we say he is lion-hearted. There was an English king who was like this. He was called Richard the Lion-hearted.

When we listen to the beating heart of man, it is as though we could hear, in this beating, the footsteps of God.

Now we know that the eagle rules in the head of man, the lion in the heart, and the bull in the limbs. But in man, too, there dwells an angel, and this angel changes the fiercenesss of the beasts so that in head and heart and limb there can live the love of God. So we can be swift and brave and strong; quick to learn and understand, gentle and loving, and eager to serve.

My dear children, all the beasts of the world can teach man something, for every beast carries a secret of God. When we learn to understand these secrets, we are also learning about God.

Now you will understand why the ox and the ass were also present at the Christmas Crib. Not only did kings and shepherds seek the Child, but the ox and the ass were also there to protect Him with their warm breath. Why the ox and the ass? They are called beasts of burden; they are the servants of man. Behind them we may think of the whole animal kingdom waiting on man. The patient ox, the lowly ass, the gentle sheep, stand very close to us. One day they will be followed by all the other creatures – but first, we must learn to understand them.'

*   *   *   *   *   *   *

We owe much to the science of our times, but just as Shylock, in demanding his pound of flesh, forgot the blood, so does modern science, in dealing with nature, forget the spirit. Such a science can never nourish the deeper forces of the human soul. An unspiritual science that leaves the heart cold, that makes demands on the intelligence but has nothing to say to the moral being of man, can never be a basis for true education. It separates man from the world and makes him an unsocial spectator. An imaginative-perceptual view of life such as has been indicated here, a view to which we have been led by Rudolf Steiner, releases the heart forces, brings warmth, enthusiasm and purpose into life, penetrates beneath the surface of the senses to the moral grounds of all existence, and unites the being of man with Nature. What the children have *enjoyed* through such a method of teaching becomes the driving force in their own endeavours in later years.

The First Approach to Physics

In a Rudolf Steiner School any approach to Nature finds its starting-point in man himself. Thus, in the first animal period in the fourth class, we can show how the various animal types that surround man present one-sided aspects of his total being. A young child whose imagination has not been spoilt can have a vivid enjoyment of the picture forms which the animals present so expressively, and can in that way come to a feeling of understanding sympathy for the animals which goes deeper than words, and which will only later flower into thoughts. From the 'form' of man we pass to the particularized 'forms' of the animal world. These animal forms are like single letters. Man, however, as he stands before us, is a revelation of the 'Word'; he alone, therefore, carries within him the seed of fully conscious experience.

In the fifth class (children aged 11) we come to that kingdom which reaches up towards the animal world. In the plant kingdom it is not the isolated 'forms', but the *progress of form* that is most important. In the plant we behold the 'unfolding' of life; that which the single plant achieves as it progresses from seed to shoot, to leaf, to blossom, is also the achievement of the plant kingdom in its entirety. Thus the mosses and lichens are plants which have remained in the first stages only. The ferns are leaf from end to end. In the dandelion the ring of leaves that spread humbly on the ground surrounds the single stem that grows up from their midst to be crowned at last with the golden flower. In later plants, we see the leaves winding their way up the stem, growing ever more delicate and refined, to pour their secret striving into the fast-shut bud, the magic casket from which, like a second birth, there is to come the crowning glory of the whole plant. This glory we see pass away into the hidden powers of

the waiting seeds, that must bide their time in the darkness of
Mother Earth until a new season of sun-filled light and warmth
shall call them forth to life and being. That which is 'unfolding
life' in the plant, Rudolf Steiner relates in its progressive stages
to the 'unfolding life of soul' in the human being. As the child
is led from stage to stage of plant life, seeing in these successive
stages a revelation of plant being, he may come to feel how, in
his own soul life, he too passes from stage to stage of knowing,
feeling, understanding. And thus the higher plants and all that is
the seed process itself is left until he has passed through puberty
to a greater maturity of soul and being. Then what he has learnt
to feel in a childlike way will flash up within him as inner power
of understanding.

It is not until the children have reached the age of 12 – the age
which is like an early or false dawn of the rise of intellectual
consciousness when feeling perception passes over to a life in
ideas – it is not till then that the child is introduced to the mineral
kingdom and to the 'pure' sciences so-called. The first of these is
physics.

It is tacitly assumed that science deals with reality. Well, a
shadow is a reality; but the man who casts the shadow is a higher
reality. In our ordinary scientific thinking it is just this higher
reality, man himself, that is designedly left out of account. It is
this that has made science as we have it, a spiritless, god-void,
shadow of reality. The truth of this is slowly dawning on the
modern mind. Human existence is something incalculable, and a
kind of science that limits itself of purpose to the calculable only
can never grasp it. We, however, have to educate human beings
and not merely clever, calculating minds. Science, therefore, if
it is to help human beings to grow and develop, must learn to
include the human being in its statement of Nature and not to
exclude him. Rudolf Steiner put it forward as a fundamental point
of practice in his art of education that the human being should
always stand centrally within the subject taught, no matter what
the subject may be. Science in our schools should bring man
closer to an understanding of his own humanity. A child of 12
is still sufficiently alive in his experience to want to clothe every

concept brought to him with flesh and blood, He can, if forced to it, mechanically learn by heart bare concepts and definitions. He can also, for example, learn to build pretence structures with meccano sets, and he may even derive pleasure from doing so. This alone, however, will merely train him to develop a kind of thinking which will come to pieces before the realities of life, like the meccano set itself. It will never enable him to enter into the nature of things. As human beings, however, we long to enter into the nature of things – that is the driving force of our being and of all human ideals. We need to transcend the obvious; not to do so is to perish as regards our pure humanity, and that is what the world is in danger of doing. Again and again, by present standards, we seek to apply 'obvious means' for solving the problems that meet us, and we fail because we miss the underlying realities within these problems.

How then are we to educate human beings to a deeper grasp of the realities? The answer is that we must restore to science that which was arbitrarily cast out at the dawn of our modern age – we must introduce qualitative values into science whilst paying due regard to the quantitative. We must include in our scientific data 'the redness of the rose' and not talk merely of wavelengths that produce an impression of red on the human retina. 'Wavelength' is not a reality, but only hypothetical notion which provides a useful basis for calculation. From such calculation we arrive at number relationships between unknowables. Such statements are not infrequent today. Science, however, is destined to lead men to insight, to 'knowing', and not merely to calculations about unknowables. The fact that these calculations, when applied to practice in limited spheres, often lead to predicable results still leaves man out of account. It still leaves him gambling away his manhood for doubtful gains. If we are to enable him to strengthen his manhood, to heighten his power of consciousness, to enliven his being, making him more capable to cope with himself and with life in general, we must evolve a scientific method which holds fast to the human sense of reality and does not skirt round it. The younger the child, the more is this vitally necessary. Physics for our 12-year-old must mean an enhancement and not a deadening of experience. It must fill him with awe and wonder and joy at the grandeur of God's plan in big and in small. If we start from 'quality', we shall also find the right place for 'quantity'. If, however, we follow the way of the modern textbook, building only on the notions of quantity to the exclusion of quality in human experience, we are lost.

By way of illustration, we will give in what follows an introduction to the world of sound for children in the sixth class. The language used for the children would naturally be different and the descriptions greatly enlarged. Moreover, the subject would be so presented as to evoke questions and answers from the children themselves.

We detect sounds in Nature with definite organs, the ears. These organs are not there apart from the world of sound. They have been evolved and created according to the laws that prevail in the realm of sound to be in harmony with those laws. Therefore, if we look at the human ear, and if we later study the whole structure of the ear, outer, middle and inner, we have visibly before us an expression of the hidden powers of the world of sound working formatively in Nature. The ears are themselves the creations of the world of sound.

We do not merely detect sounds with our ears, we are affected by the sounds we hear. There are sounds that are soothing and harmonizing, sounds that please us, and there are sounds which grate on us and disturb us. Our feelings are directly taken hold of by what we hear. Our ears therefore are intermediaries between a creative world outside and our own hidden life of soul.

We ourselves are largely created by the sounds that surround us from our birth. The different languages, by their sounds, have a very definite influence on the way human beings grow up. For example, a child of Russian parents brought up on the English language will be very much 'Englished' in the process. So, too, refined speech or coarse speech has a determining effect on child development even down to the bodily appearance. Coarse language will tend to coarsen the appearance of the child as it grows, refined language will have a refining effect. We can also quote the remarkable instance of a child born of dumb parents and therefore deprived of the influence of coherent language in his early stages of development. The child in his demeanour was vague, loose, unformed, incoherent, weak in character, lacking in will and self-determination.

What are the sounds we hear around us? There are the sounds of wind and wave, the rustling of leaves, the babbling of the brook, the rolling of a dislodged rock, the patter of raindrops, the sharp tapping of hailstones, the rumbling of thunder. This is a language that takes hold of the outsides of things – it is a world of inanimate sound. Mingling with it are the sounds of the hammer, the saw, the hum of a wheel, the sound of tools, instruments, engines, plied or driven by the power of man. The kingdom of the plants unless moved from outside is a world as silent as that of the minerals. We may hear a branch snap, a tree crash down – these are still mechanical sounds caused from outside. Closely associated with the plant kingdom, however, is the world of the insects. Here, in the hum and buzz and flutter of the insect world, a new world of sound bears in on the first. The insects produces their characteristic sounds. Even these, however, on examination, prove to be mechanical in their nature. The world of sound has here gripped the living world but still only from the outside.

It is only when we come to the higher animals, the vertebrates, beginning with the croak of the frog, the hiss of the serpent, the song of the bird, and the various calls and cries of the mammalian creatures, that we encounter for the first time a world of sound born from within – sounds of joy, of pain, of fear, of the call for companionship, the ewe bleating for her lamb, and so on. Here for the first time we meet sound as a language of soul, sound formed from inner, non-spatial realms. We soon come to see how each type of organism is fashioned for the sound it emits. Out of the silent world of the invertebrates we come to the sounding world of the vertebrates. When we hear the bursting into song of the birds, it is as though Nature herself were bursting into song, rejoicing at her great achievement. We may begin to see that all the sounds we have heard before are mere reflections, echoes, of the inwardness of sound: thus, even the wind and the waves and the babbling brooks may appear to us to be 'ensouled'.

But now into this miraculous world of sound, sound born of the invisible world of soul, doleful sounds, eerie sounds, hungry sounds, angry sounds, joyous sounds, the sound of the lover calling to his mate, the dam calling to her young – into this world of single cries and utterances emitted by the several creatures there enters the kingdom of the meaningful word, the shining through of reason, of the human spirit, the language of conscious endeavour, of human intercourse, of revelation from being to being. It is a language of communion in higher spheres of experience. The Word more than anything else declares man to be a member of a kingdom of his own within the rest of nature. Whereas the animal in its cry is given over to the particular emotion that fills it, language is that which informs the soul, which rules and directs the soul from still greater depths of being.

As surely as language is infinitely more than the sum total of the natural cries of animals, so surely is the music composed by man something immeasurably greater than the loveliest singing of the birds. It is born from another source, and evolves from stage to stage with the evolving nature of man. We think of 'Orpheus with his lute' singing to the accompaniment of his own music, singing of the mysteries of world-creation and world-event. Who but a mind deadened to dust by materialistic theories can fail to see in man an order of being standing within Nature, and yet distinct from all that surrounds him, singing immortal songs, despite his mortal frame.

Returning to the animals, we can discriminate between the different kinds of sounds. The cry of the eagle, the king of the birds, appears to us as a shrill piercing head-cry; the roar of the lion with its rumbling breath proceeds from its mighty chest; the bellow of the bull filled with inner fire bursts forth from deep below the diaphragm. We can thus begin to locate the sounds and to appreciate their quality according to their place of origin. In this way we are led over to a first consideration of the nature of 'pitch' in sounds.

To begin with, the tiny child makes marvellously high sounds; as it grows more and more into its bodily nature, as the body increases, so the sounds become deeper, more earthly. The sounds appear to descend gradually from higher spheres; as the body increases the pitch falls. In human beings many other factors play in. The simplicity of the law is revealed by a visit to the organ of the nearest church. Here we see at a glance the relationship between pitch and physical dimension, the bigger the pipe the lower the pitch. In the violin the strings are of the same length, but they differ in thickness – it is the same law of matter in another form; as matter increases, so the pitch falls, until, to return to the organ again, musical tone fades off into what is little more than physical vibration. In the piano strings, we can see the combination of length and thickness as the physical basis for varying pitch.

We can advance now to the study of the musical scale. We can, for example, take vessels of the same height and by filling them with water to different levels examine the pitch produced by the different vibrating air-columns. We can examine the stops of a musical pipe and see how this principle of the length of the air-column determines the position of the different holes.

We can next proceed by making use of the mono-chord, and discover how the different intervals in music are related to the numerical ratios in the lengths of the vibrating chords. We can show also what we mean by the vibrations of strings. For example, with the help of little riders placed along a vibrating string, we can soon discover the nodes or points of rest and the points of greatest amplitude; at the former, the rider remains on the string, at the latter it is immediately shot off.

Thus we come down eventually to number relationships; simple ratios produce harmonious intervals, complicated ratios express disharmonies. We discover that music, the most tangible of the human experiences that reach us through the senses, must conform to exact mathematical laws of ratio if it is to find expression in the realm of matter. We have thus 'come to earth' with our subject.

It makes all the difference to a growing child, as indeed it does to all of us, whether we say that sounds are produced by vibrating strings or columns of air, or whether we say that sound manifests wherever the laws of its being are reflected in the mathematical ratios that govern the vibration of physical objects. The former statement closes the way to further enquiry – it shuts the door on the spirit. The latter opens ways for further investigation, ways that led Pythagoras to his teaching of the music of the spheres.

Here, then, is an example of the way in which physics may first be introduced to young children. Beginning with the qualitative experiences in which man has his being, we can lead to an even more alive grasp of the quantitative laws expressed in mathematical ratios bound to matter. It opens the way to a study of number ratios as reflections of heavenly events. It places man centrally between the world of matter and the mysteries that rule his being, so that he can look up from the earth to the world of the stars and the circling planets and see creation as an outer manifestation of the divine spirit. This stirs the imagination and fortifies the will. Nothing has been lost of the exactitude of discovered law, but immeasurably much has been gained for the growth of human experience. In this way science can provide a means for the education of man and not merely an exercise for the frozen intellect. Whoever has had the experience of teaching young children in the way here indicated will know how it can engender strength and courage and enthusiasm for life in contrast to the nightmare of universal fear, distrust and frustration that fills the columns of every daily newspaper throughout the world today. We have to educate so that we may free the human spirit from its bondage to matter.

The physics of the sixth class includes a similar study of light, of heat, and of static electricity. All these subjects are extended through the seventh and eight classes, and to them are added current electricity, mechanics, and the growth of industry with the discovery of power machines. The children are not left in fairyland, but are led to the workshops, the station-yards and the factories. In the Upper School all this is carried a good deal further. Nevertheless, the character of the teaching remains the same. Only a science that does not shrink from including in its data the qualitative experiences of the human soul can advance to modes of thought, perception and discovery that can bring the healing of the spirit to a harassed mankind.

The Teaching of Religion
at a Rudolf Steiner School

What is your attitude to religion? This question comes generally at the end of the interview. The inquiring parent wishes to be assured that the religious instruction given at the school will not separate his child from his home upbringing. For most parents the briefest possible answer seems to be sufficient: 'Religion lessons are given regularly throughout the school. The teaching is definitely Christian but not sectarian'. There are some, however, with strong convictions of their own who wish for a fuller answer, and others again who would frankly prefer there to be no religious instruction: 'Why not leave the children free to make up their own minds when they grow up?'

It is the common view that education has to do with matters of knowledge and general upbringing and that religion is a personal affair of the home. A formal inspection of a school does not include the religion teaching unless the headmaster (in our case the College of Teachers) wishes it. This in itself shows that religion is regarded as something additional to a school curriculum and not necessarily as part of it. In any case, by religion lessons most people mean Scripture lessons which could very well be given at a Sunday School.

In a Rudolf Steiner School we make a distinction between religious devotion and the profession of a particular faith. All human culture, not only religion but art, philosophy, healing, rulership and social law has, until recent times, had its roots in the soil of religious devotion. 'No Bishop, no King', is a last echo of a view of life that dates back to the Pharaohs, the Priest-kings of Egypt, and even further. Religion, therefore, is inseparable from any true study of history. Since, in our view, childhood is a recapitulation of all the essential experiences of the human race, and since religious devotion has been a most powerful formative force in human history and culture, to rob the child of this experience is to deny him something that properly belongs to his growing years. Far from leaving the child free by denying him this, we put him at the mercy of the adult scepticism common today. The mood of religious devotion strengthens the moral forces in childhood and helps to establish character. Scepticism, on the other hand, is built on negation and by this very fact tends to breed an attitude of uncertainty towards life. It will be admitted that modern religious scepticism has spread through the world in recent centuries as a product of the abstract intellect. The young child is not an intellectual and cannot think abstractly – if he does, he has been torn out of his childhood too soon to his lasting detriment; abstract thought only begins to come into its own with adolescence and even then, if development has been healthy, it is so permeated with natural enthusiasms and a secret hungering for the heroic that it is not at all the bloodless intellectualism of the disillusioned adult. To bring religious devotion to the young is not to leave them unfree; but rather is it to make them healthy. Religious dogmas leave the soul unfree but not religious devotion.

Religion lessons in Steiner Schools are not confined to the Scriptures though they include them. Christ said: 'I am come to fulfil the law'. We must therefore try to understand the law. Law, as it expressed itself in bygone ages, made no distinction as yet between jurisdiction and moral religious law. This is true not only of the law of the Hebrews but of all peoples. We must therefore take pre-Christian culture seriously in all its grandeur and in all its varied expressions as preparation for the Advent of Christ. So, too, with natural law. The language of the modern textbook is as remote from living nature as the dissection of a corpse from the living inspiration of the poet. Nature has a language of her own for the human soul; her beauty and her tenderness, her terror and sublimity call forth reverence, awe, devotion and love – moods that played powerfully into the childhood of the race and that belong equally to the childhood of today. Nature has ever claimed her rightful place in the devotional life of man. Those two aspects of life, that of history and that of nature, flow together into religious experience. It follows, therefore, that the religion teaching in such a school cannot be merely segregated from all the rest of the teaching; the religion lessons seek rather to find religious expression for that which permeates the whole of the education as the ideals of manhood. These lessons are completely integrated into the rest of the school life; on the other hand, were there no specific religion lessons, the religious element would still not be lacking, for it is inwoven in the art, the science, the history and all else that is taught in the school.

From the above it will be clear that the Christianity we mean is something all-human and all-embracing that cannot conflict with any particularized aspect of it. On the other hand, adherence to a particular church or denomination belongs properly to the home and not at all to the school.

We have given the broad character of the religion teaching in our schools. What of the content of the lessons? What makes the religion teaching specifically Christian?

Christian teaching has its centre in the Mystery of the Holy Trinity. Is there anything in common experience that we can relate to this mystery? If we can, then this will give us the basis we seek.

The adult can look back over his life. In the first place, he finds himself a being within Nature. He knows that to be there at all he had to have earthly parents. He knows that the building of the body he now bears was plunged in profoundest unconsciousness. Nature evolved him and bore him along from stage to stage, from conception to birth, and then after birth through all the succeeding phases of childhood. This whole process with its inevitable lawfulness completely escapes his conscious grasp. Even as an adult, all that sustains him from day to day, all that carries him through every sleeping into every waking, all that maintains him in bodily existence, his breathing, his circulation, his metabolism, the very condition of his consciousness that enables him to think – all this is, for the greater part, beyond his knowing and volition.

He is immersed in Nature, himself a part of Nature. He knows also that out of the unconscious condition of early infancy and childhood he gradually emerged into consciousness.

In the process of wakening from early childhood he began little by little to become cognizant of himself. His memory extends back to a certain moment, the moment when he was first able to utter the word 'I' to himself. Rudolf Steiner has again and again drawn attention to the peculiar place this single word occupies in the whole language. Everything else can be learnt by imitation. Every John begins by calling himself John, every Mary by calling herself Mary. We cannot, however, address ourselves as 'I' by imitation. Here there is a kind of leap. Something must rise up like a sudden intuition, a flash of consciousness from within, and for the rest of life this that rises up 'from within' enables us to say the word 'I'. To this magical point, magical in the sense that it transcends a mere nature process, extends our memory within which we hold the sum total of our personal experiences. We grasp ourselves in person. Gradually from this moment we begin to build up an inner life all of our own. As childhood proceeds, particularly in the middle years (the class-teacher age), we can begin to enter more and more into our own dreams and imagination. We become aware of an inner world, a life of soul that is our very own.

We can thus make a clear distinction between that which brings us here unconsciously on the path of Nature and this emergence of an inner and personal content to our lives. We are all equally a part of Nature, but we are each something special to ourselves.

There is a particular moment in childhood when this discovery of the 'self' is sharply accentuated. It occurs in the ninth to the tenth year. This is like a second phase of the birth of 'I'. If the episode of the third year flashes into consciousness like an intuition, this later phase is accompanied by a deepening of the 'feeling' life. For the first time the child begins to know the real meaning of loneliness, of being alone with himself in a world that is forever outside. It is the beginning of the inevitable gulf that widens out between the self as subject and the world as the object of our contemplation. Equally, we may say from this moment we become increasingly an object to ourselves. Hitherto the child has lived more or less at one with his surroundings and himself; now there is the beginning of this division. This first beginning of 'self-awareness', of being alone with oneself, remains throughout life. Here, for the first time, questions begin to form themselves as regards personal destiny. As the years proceed, these feelings and questionings become more defined. Something comes to expression within us which we can never derive from Nature alone, something that feels itself to be a stranger in this world. Life becomes a riddle.

But there is a further phase. From the moment that we begin to know ourselves as distinct from others, we also become more clearly aware of these others. We can no longer take their connection with us simply for granted. The adolescent especially is concerned with the question of human relationships. Life has no meaning if we merely live for ourselves. Human beings are interdependent and interconnected. What is the true basis of companionship in life? In earlier epochs and also in childhood today there is the direct dependence on blood relationship. Gradually the soul emancipates itself from this. We wish to build up relationships on the basis of mutual understanding. In this modern age we may feel more akin to a stranger and a foreigner than to our own brother. We strive to build up our connections with others, to achieve a community of interests with our fellow men, a community by choice and not by necessity.

Here, then, are three clear phases of human experience well known to us all: we never quite outgrow the first, we never completely penetrate the second, we never fully achieve the third. The intellect may make us aware but something far deeper must stir in us if we are to come nearer to all that is expressed in this common unfolding of every human life.

In Christian terms we might now say: this coming into being on the path of Nature, this resting within Nature and being sustained by Nature beyond our knowing, this is an echo of the Mystery of the Father God, the ground of all existence, in Whom we rest and have our being. Here is the greatest mystery of all. The feeling that can fill us in contemplation of the Father God is one of infinite gratitude for the past and for all that surrounds us that is born of the past. Here is the true ground of Faith.

In this world of being we find our own being, we come to realize our 'self'. This is something that is not merely given but that is constantly evolving from within. All through life a man may continue to develop and as he does so the circle of his interests grows ever wider. What is this expanding self? Nature is sinless, but here we confront the problem of sin, for the experience of self can turn to self-seeking, to egotism. We are brought into a condition of strife with ourselves till we begin to realize that to find his true self man must overcome his everyday self. Christ, who lived and died selflessly, becomes the God whom we aspire. As St. Paul said: 'Not I but Christ in me'. Through Christ we may overcome the temptation of egotism, the Fall through Lucifer. Infinite love must fill us as we contemplate the deed of suffering of Christ for the salvation of the human soul. In Him we find the true I AM, the working of the Son God, the Second Person of the Trinity. He is the true fount of Love, of Charity.

Christ entered the realm of Nature to make Himself one with Nature. 'I and the Father are One'. He entered the kingdom of man to make Himself one with all men. 'I am with you always'. He is ever present in our midst. 'Before Abraham was I AM'. He is the Healer and the Inspirer of Human Culture from all time and His kingdom extends into the future. 'I am the Alpha and the Omega'. He not only died but He rose again. Those who receive Him are Christened in His name. They take His immortality into themselves. He said: 'I will send you my Comforter, the Spirit of Truth'. Nature separates men into races, nations, families, many tongues. All this is necessary that men may grow differentiated from one another. This process left to itself must lead to the condition of each against all, division and division and further division such as is happening today. Those who die to themselves to be reborn in Christ have that in them through which men may grow united again. This is what happened at the Pentecost. The Word declared itself through the single mouths of men, not in one tongue but in many tongues. Each has his own spirit, but through

Christ, at the Pentecost experience, there descended into each man the Fire of the World Spirit, the Holy Spirit, the Third Person of the Trinity. It happened once, but it can happen again and again, 'Where two or three are gathered in My name'. Here lives the hope for the future. Here is the basis for the new community, not the community by blood, but the community by the inflow of the Holy Spirit. Thus will men learn to be servants of the Word all the world over, in faith, in charity, in perfect understanding. As man bears the possibility of these three within him and is destined to express all three, so are the Three in One and the One in Three.

What I have attempted to express are the ideals that underlie the religion lessons, vary as they will for the different years. What matters most is that we should bring about the right mood. With the younger children we shall speak in such a way that they may have the feeling: Nature is the gift of God and the powers of man are also the gift of God; the whole of life comes to us as a great, a beneficent gift. Here is expressed devotion to the Father principle – it calls forth reverence in the human soul.

In the third class (children aged 9) the children are told the Old Testament stories, not in the religion lessons but in their main lessons. These stories meet them at the critical moment described above when they need special reassurance and increased confidence. A sense of destiny pervades all these stories. We see how step by step man has to take the responsibility for himself on to his own shoulders, but always to fulfil a greater task, one that can serve his fellow men. At this time, too, to meet this first awakening to the 'personal', we may begin to introduce stories about Jesus. These can be supplemented by stories of the Saints. Much may be done later with biographies – the life of Francis of Assisi, the life of Helen Keller, and so on – to show how human life can express itself in the most varied ways, in the overcoming of obstacles for the achievement of a greater good. In the seventh and eighth classes we may begin a more consecutive study of the Gospels; in the life of Christ, the sacrifice of Christ and His victory, we see the archetype of all true living: we are filled with devotion and love in contemplating His Being.

Coming into the Upper School, when the children leave their

class teacher and find themselves 'alone', a most fitting theme
will be the Acts of the Apostles: also the life of St. Augustine
and the way he had to struggle through to his faith. In the tenth
class we may enlarge on the journeys of St. Paul with reference
to the Epistles showing how the central experience of his life
on the road to Damascus had to find the most varied forms
of expression for the different communities through which he
moved. We might also take the life of Buddha in the East, with
his teaching of compassion and that of Socrates in the West,
with his search for wisdom, to show how from opposite sides
they were both precursors of that which was to find fulfilment
in the Christ Event. Confidence in life, courage for the truth, can
fill us as we see such diversity resolved into a higher union of
experience. Truth is more than opinion – here speaks the language
of the Holy Spirit. Devotion to truth, courage for the truth, meets
us as the third ideal.

In the eleventh class much space is given in the main lessons
to the teaching of the Grail and all that this has meant for
the succeeding centuries right into the nineteenth century – for
example, the poems of Tennyson and Wagner's *Parsifal*. In the
Arthurian legends, Whitsuntide is a specially Holy Day, when
the knights would not sit down to meat until there came some
messenger, some wonder of the Spirit. In the nourishing by means
of the Grail there lives the Mystery of the transubstantiation, the
forces of the Resurrection, for the forming of community in the
Spirit. These and kindred subjects can fill the religion lessons,
too. The works of Shakespeare show an immense achievement
in this direction. There is much concealed Christianity in a poem
like 'Prometheus Unbound'. The whole impulse towards freedom
carries within it the quest for a true communion between man
and man. The realization of this leads to a sense of blessedness
streaming towards us from the future.

Finally, in the twelfth class, the children are given a survey of
all the great religions of the human race and are led towards an
understanding of the evolutionary possibilities within Christianity
itself. With this they leave us to enter into life.

What has been outlined above is not a set syllabus but is

intended only to indicate the trend of the religion lessons through the different years of school life. Each religion teacher is free to select what he thinks best suited for his children. Each will draw on his own life experience and his own powers of interpretation.

As a background to the whole teaching year by year there is the life of the seasons and the recurring Christian festivals. Christmas, the festival of birth, is a festival for old and young alike. Most parents will have experienced the Advent festivals for the youngest children leading up to the Christmas plays which the teachers perform annually for the whole school. The Easter festival, with its message of death and resurrection as distinct from the resurrection of Nature in the spring-time, is reserved for the children in the Upper School. Whitsuntide is not celebrated as a festival for it can be approached by the oldest children only. On the other hand, the Midsummer festival, closing with the scene of the lighting of the St. John's fire, is an occasion that brings back many old scholars and their parents to renew their connections with the school. Finally, at the beginning of every school year, there is the Michaelmas festival, when Nature is passing over into death, but the spirit in man wakens the more strongly to its own life. Thus, the rhythm of the year acquires a deepened and a hallowed meaning that echoes on through all the years. The Christian festivals occurring at the different seasons of the year educate in man the sense that, standing within nature, he nevertheless lives by a higher law: 'My Kingdom is not of this world'.

In the end we may say there is no aspect of life that cannot be reviewed and rediscovered in the light of religious experience. The effect of the religion teaching is to enhance human values. Every old scholar of our schools will know what it has meant to him; he will know how he left school with active interest in all that concerns man, but without bias, free to make his own discoveries, to question, dismiss, reconsider, reaffirm and, if he will, evolve further that which has been brought to him. His senses have been quickened and his heart warmed in childhood that he may the better find his way in manhood. Where this has proved true, the religion lessons have fulfilled their mission.

Eighteen – The School Leaving Age

The plan of a Rudolf Steiner School extends over twelve school years, covering the ages from 6 to 18. Of these twelve years, eight are spent with the class teacher and the remaining four in the Upper School. The question arises whether 18 is a real age for leaving school or an arbitrary one. This question is not confined to Steiner schools. Most of the better-known schools in Great Britain have held to this age; so do the grammar schools now approximately. The older universities have favoured this age for College Entrance; many professions and industries, both for men and women, plan their training to begin at 18; during the days of national service, it and, in war time, compulsory service, commenced at 18. Why then 18?

Anyone familiar with the workings of a Steiner school will know that each year of the twelve has a character of its own. The Nursery Class lives apart. Education proper begins with the first class. It then proceeds year by year, the work being assembled each year anew to meet the particular phase of development of that year. It is the general development that is of primary importance, so that the chronological age alone determines the grouping of the children and never the so-called mental age.

In the class-teacher period, the rule is Authority. The authority of the class teacher as he accompanies his group of children through the eight years is the central directing force that works through the community of the class – an authority based on loving understanding and growing knowledge of the children. Then, at 14, this is suddenly withdrawn. The child, on entering the Upper School, faces a quite different situation. There is no

104

such central, personal authority any longer. Instead he confronts, in each teacher, an authority in a given subject. Each teacher, however, is at the same time a representative of the collective body of teachers – the College of Teachers. Each, in his own way, brings towards him that which inspires the work of the whole school. This is rarely expressed in words. The child discovers it – not all at once, but progressively as he matures. In a personal way he will probably feel more connected with some teachers than with others; there will certainly be some teachers who never teach him at all – yet they, too, form an integral part of the collective picture that surrounds him – they too are members of the College of Teachers. It is the community of teachers that now constitutes for him the authority of the school; as regards personal loyalties he is left free.

At the same time, from the moment he enters the Upper School, he is differently membered within the community of his own class. He and his classmates have been left to themselves. Only that which transpires between them can now maintain the unity of the class – not a teacher. Individual relationships play themselves out and may change. The class, however, is something more: it acquires a character, a tone, of its own – it is a collective entity like the College of Teachers, a community patterned on a community within the greater community of the school.

It is in this social setting that the child, rapidly becoming a young man or woman, ripens in understanding for the world he is to enter, if he completes his education at 18.

A Steiner education, viewing childhood as the progressive entry of a soul and spirit into a bodily nature, must pay special heed to the subtleties and changing undertones from year to year. Subjects are introduced and selected accordingly. This cannot be arbitrary. Healthy development is the first concern: knowledge is made subservient to human need. The child, being many-sided, requires the many-sidedness of a College to meet him; hence the practice of weekly college meetings where the endeavour is 'to learn from one another'. Through this fact the work attains objectivity whilst retaining all its human warmth.

Experience has shown that at 14 to 15 children have a natural sympathy for all the great pioneers and discoverers who led the way out of mediaevalism into modern times. The child's impulse to assert his own independence here finds support in history. The first great enterprises in science and industry, the emergence of the power machine, the redistribution of population into cities, the French Revolution, the Industrial Revolution in England, the American War of Independence, the search for an 'ideal community' – these and similar themes are specially in accord with the sympathies and interests of children in the ninth class.

In the tenth class (age 16) interest broadens to 'world outlook'. Is not mankind on earth an all-inclusive community? In what way are nations and peoples interdependent? What constitutes the body of the earth? How does the history of the world proceed? What constitutes the body of man? How does the human spirit dwell within it? What are the great ideals of the human race? What is the meaning and essence of poetry? What is love? What is the mission of science? The 16-year-old wants to understand the world as it is. He is eager to appreciate what the world has to offer, to admire and emulate the achievements of the human race, to extol the modern age. He loves and enjoys material existence. He is a hearty realist.

In the eleventh class, at 17, the mood changes. Children are affected differently, some hardly at all, and some acutely. The root question now is not so much 'How' as 'Why?' The state of the world is fairly plain. There are contradictions everywhere and these provoke questions of another kind. Is religion true? Have ideals any meaning? What about Hiroshima? Is man moving in a more or less blind drift or has he a real part to play? These doubts struggle with the longing for positive answers. But what positive answers can the adult give to make life seem worthwhile? Youth has a natural zest for living but there is often real despondency. Much, at this stage, depends on the home. It is now that the character of a Steiner education begins to speak in the child himself. The whole education, above all in its treatment of history, strives to develop an evolutionary sense from within. Against this background the Grail Saga has quite special meaning. The real idealist is seen to be the only true realist. It is the ideals in manhood that are the motive powers to move nations and the world. It is these that distinguish man from nature. It becomes *obvious* that human progress comes through sacrifice – the sacrifice of individuals who care for their ideals more than they do for themselves. All through the story of man, wherever there has been a potent negative, there have been those who have asserted a greater positive. The human world has not gone under, for in every crisis the spirit of man has proved unconquerable. For this spirit, opposition is the springboard to achievement. It is in danger and distress that the hero in man shines forth most brightly, and this has been proved times without number. Whether it is history, geography, literature, art, botany, astronomy – all subjects rally to a common call – to assert that there is truth, that there is love, that there is redemption, that there is fellowship, that there is a City of God.

In the 18-year-old the heart is awake. Whatever the head may assemble as evidence, judgement springs from the heart. Whether men agree or disagree does not depend on evidence alone, for that can be the same for both; nor does it depend on intelligence alone, for they may be of equal intelligence. With the same evidence and with equal intelligence, they may form quite opposite judgements. Were this not so, there never would be heretics, and without heretics there never would be progress. According to Rudolf Steiner, original judgement can only begin from about 18 years of age. At 18 the mind is able to survey wide vistas – to comprehend a point from the circumference rather than be always looking outwards from a point. This is an aim of the education, to view the world as a whole and to perceive the parts within the whole – to view mankind as a whole and to perceive one's own part within that whole. Only then can there be true compassion for another.

Nothing relates to the awakened 18-year-old more than a play like *The Tempest*, a record of frailties, of treacheries, but also of redeeming sacrifice springing from the wide, comprehensive view of Prospero – a tale in the end of reconciliation and of a new-born sense of community. The strong are the compassionate: the weak revive new hopes. Nor is man alone in Nature: he has his companion kingdoms that surround him and sustain him, lending stature to his being. In ordinary life, the lesser bows to the greater. In spiritual life the reverse is true: there the greatest have ever humbled themselves before the least, as in the Washing of the Feet. Thus do stone and plant and beast enter into the community of man, and it is thus that these subjects are introduced and presented for study. This does not contradict the sciences but gives them meaning – it makes knowledge, acquired by the head, into an affair of the heart. As the sun is the quickener of outer nature, so is there a fountain of light, a source of warmth within man, which quickens his inner life, urging him to grow beyond himself – to become his true self. If the preceding years have met with their answers truly, then in the 18-year-old there shines forth a new quality of appreciation, a new trust and confidence, a wonderful friendliness towards the world. He has found confirmation for himself that there is truth in life, and he is ready to set out to handle his earthly tasks for spiritual ends.

It is now he is ready to leave school, to spend his last protected years before he comes of age in free movement amongst his fellows. Now the world becomes his extended school, be it at the university, in the professions, in the forces, or wherever his life should lead him. He steps out into the street to seek his place within the community of man. This he may do now, for he carries the core of his manhood within him, and he will not easily suffer defeat. To borrow an image from Rudolf Steiner, he is ready to stride through the necessities of life on the road to inner freedom.

There is a law closely observed in Rudolf Steiner Schools – it is that *form* proceeds from the head towards the limbs, always in three main stages. In the embryo it is first the head and then the heart and then the limbs that make their appearance. This sequence continues after birth. In the first seven years up to the change of teeth it is the bodily organs mainly that are formed and perfected. In the second life-period up to adolescence, the formative process turns inwards, the life functions are established, the innate capacities are revealed. In the adolescent it is above all the understanding that is formed.

In the first stage of adolescence, understanding is mainly in the head. The child looks out with new interest and enquiry. In the middle years of adolescence, from 16 to 18, this spirit of inquiry descends to the heart. Questioning about the world deepens into a questioning about the meaning of life and human destiny. Beyond 18, the urge to explore descends into the limbs and becomes an urge to move on – to learn about the world by moving through it. Thus 18 appears to be the right and natural age for leaving school.

Life is the quest for man. The task of education is to prepare for this. The last phase of education from 18 to 21 leads the young person into the world. At 21 the adult is born. Then, in the truest sense, education ceases and self-education begins.

Teacher, Doctor and Farmer

*The following address was given at a Biodynamic Conference at
Emerson College in January 1986.*

I don't know why they've asked me to speak here, I'm not a
farmer, but during the war I did work a small piece of land
myself. I planted vegetables and they grew, and I put potatoes in
the earth as they should be; in fact is was a very enjoyable work.
That's all I know, that the vegetables did respond to treatment
– that has not always been my experience as a teacher. There's
quite a remarkable difference between vegetables and people –
vegetables know what to do if you know what to do. With
people you are sure you know, but they never do! It's really
very difficult.

So I asked myself what am I to speak about that isn't
theoretical, at least for me. I'll tell you what I want to speak
about from the very beginning. That's why we have a farm
here. I've been repeating for years and years that there's no
education of the human being in the real sense unless there is
co-operation between teacher, doctor and farmer, To be able to
bring people into the world so that they *can* meet the situations
that they meet today, we need the intimate co-operation of these
three. I don't think that has fully arisen. So that's what I'd like to
talk about.

Now I've been told that it's to be a short talk, but to make it
short I'd have to talk very, very quickly. I don't intend to do
that. But I do want to introduce this very seriously because I
don't think it has been fully grasped. In our Waldorf education
work we know that we have a head and we have to do something
about that. We know that we have a middle sphere. But we forget

that we have a third system. You see, Rudolf Steiner added to the words 'know thyself' which were inscribed over the temple of Apollo; he added for today 'know thyself in body, soul and spirit'. That's the new development. So much of anthroposophy is a development of this threefold statement. A teacher cannot manage without the doctor beside him. A growing child cannot really grow as it should without the farmer right there next to him. I want to develop that a little further.

What is the task of the teacher? If we look at the threefold development of man we can say man has a nerve-sense organization; he has a rhythmic organization, that is a respiratory-circulatory organization; and he has a limb-metabolic organization. This is the most mysterious far-reaching and the deepest really to grasp. What do we mean by limb-metabolism? The task of the teacher is really in the realm of nerve/sense, in the realm of thought. His realm is particularly the ultimate goal we can read of in Rudolf Steiner's *The Philosophy of Freedom*; can the human being really relate what meets him in the world as percept with the right concept? We're endowed with faculties for perceiving what is in the world around us. How do we take hold of it? We have to bring to birth out of ourselves the corresponding thought or idea or concept. If I hold this piece of chalk up you see what it is. Previous experience may have taught you that it's a piece of chalk, but if you have not already seen a piece of chalk you might think it's a piece of anything. First of all you have to see it, to recognize it you have to see it (if your vision is faulty you won't), and then you have to have an idea which you yourself have to bring to meet it. If you have the right idea and you have grasped it, then these two things have met and you feel 'Now I've got a solid experience'. If it is the false idea then the thing falsifies and is wrong. The whole of our life is an attempt – can we really see at all? And can we bring to birth the faculty to grasp what we see, to take hold of it, unite with it? The one half is given, the other half we have to produce. So that's the task of the teacher, so to educate that human beings as they grow up in the world will have an open eye, an *interest* (without interest you see nothing at all). They must be able to perceive what meets them instead of being blank to it; they must be able to bring to birth the idea or the thought that relates to the percept. That's the task of the teacher – that human beings will be able to know themselves in the world of phenomena.

The task of the doctor is to establish a true respiration. We in-breathe and we out-breathe; and remember, when the child is born, the first act is the in-breathing. The lungs do not function in the embryo, they are contracted, they are high up, and everything depends on whether those lungs can be filled with air and descend. The breath enters into us. God breathed into Adam and then he became a living soul. That happens to every human being, to every living creature that breathes. First the in-breath and then the senses open and next the out-breath. All our life we are taking in the breath that comes to us, and we are breathing out. Our perceptions are not fine enough for us to realize that every person breathes out differently. We say that one persons speaks a different language, expresses himself in different words and images. In actual fact his breathing out is something that is penetrated with the same forces that declare themselves in the way he describes or expounds, relates himself into word.

Here we are dealing with the awareness that we are not a mixture of nitrogen, oxygen, goodness knows what, but the living breath, the breath that has life in it. The doctor has to protect that. If the in-breathing is too rapid and intense we fall ill. If the out-breathing is too shallow and indifferent we fall below par. If there's a healthy respiration going together with the circulation, if a person breathes rightly then he is alright. And that has to do very much more with our feeling life. You catch your breath or you inspire when you get a shock. So I would like to add to the doctor all that helps us to develop life of soul, everything which has to do with the world of art. It is a very special world to enter into so that it has the right balance, so that it's not too dark, too light, just balanced. You can see that in children, in the way they write. Some are too contracted, some fall off the line, others are falling backwards, others forward. If you study it you will see a sort of language there of where the child is in its disposition. Now that has to be helped, directed to find a true balance in the life of feeling. The doctor has to do it in the study of the whole organism so that there can be a right balance.

Also waking and sleeping is a kind of respiration. We breathe in the life of the soul, we breathe it out at night. Incarnation and excarnation is a kind of breathing. In incarnation we breathe in the spirit, in excarnation we breathe it out. So you see we meet on all these different levels just that question of respiration. How we take in impressions and respond to them, how we take in the breath and what we give back, and the life of soul with this.

Now, the limb/metabolism organization is the most mysterious of all. We need the fruits of Nature. What do we do with them? Is man a continuation of the food he eats? This has often been said, but he is not. The deepest mysteries of science are connected with this question. We take in the fruits of Nature and what happens? To begin with we utterly destroy them. We all do the same work of destruction if we are healthy. You know that beautiful apple that makes your mouth water – once you have swallowed it your attitude is utterly different. The first thing is that we utterly destroy that which we took in from Nature. Whilst it remains in the digestive tract it is outside us. Something has to find its way through the walls of the alimentary canal. It is full of mystery, it is not a simple chemical process at all. The analysis of what goes through is different in certain ways from what goes in. You have a milky-white fluid in the intestines, and you have a milky-white fluid on the other side, and they are different. There is a mysterious selective process, and it is in discovering this that science is so wonderful. The organism knows and receives certain things willingly and gladly, and other things it takes more cautiously or not at all. There is a kind of conscious wisdom there which can discriminate. So how do we build up again? It is not the same substance anymore. It is an original act which each one has to perform and to build up so that it is true to each one's nature: in other words so that we may maintain our form, our image. We can eat the same food all day long and every day of our lives but we still keep our own form. We have destroyed the substances by the same rules because they are external to us. The absorption, the building up to keep your likeness in the world, your absolutely individual image, that's far deeper, far more mysterious than the others, even though they are all great mysteries. Man is a mystery!

This third part; limb/metabolism, is, in my experience, the least understood, the least taken seriously enough in our schools. I am talking as a teacher now. Yes, we know how to develop the thoughts. We work with art, we know how important that is. But the food, the diet, what we put into the body out of Nature, meets with an extraordinary indifference for the most part. It does not reach. There is the classroom, the studio, eurythmy, gymnastics but the education does not reach as far as the kitchen and the connection between the kitchen and the field. That's the part that has to be developed much more.

If I translate this into spiritual language one could say in relation to Father, Son and Holy Spirit, in the body we meet the mystery of the Father, from whom we are all born. In the Soul we meet the mystery of the Son who said: 'I am in the Father and the Father is in me'. It is the Christ, the Son who said 'I will send you the Holy Spirit, the Spirit of Truth, the Comforter' through which you can begin to recognize all three mysteries, and, above all, what destiny is; and in that recognition find comfort and consolation and courage and encouragement in life instead of being like lost souls. I do not think that can be achieved except through an intimate relationship between teacher, doctor and farmer. That is why I felt we had to have a farm here, not just a place for lecture-rooms and studios. We have to have a Biodynamic farm and gardens. I had hoped that everybody who came here would have an opportunity to realize the importance of what Biodynamics is, and I want to say a word about that also from my aspect.

What is Biodynamics? What is it? I wanted everybody to have that experience because they go off to schools, to homes, to villages and communities and if they take with them that insight into what Biodynamics is then they can begin to give real service to the third man, the metabolic man. We have lots of people with good ideas, and lots of people with good feelings, but how many people do you meet who have a stern will that carries through? That is the hardest to achieve. I am not claiming to have achieved it, but I am aware of it and that it is very important.

One could go further in anthroposophy, and then one could know that the highest of the hierachies are called Spirits of Strength – Cherubim, Seraphim, Thrones. They are the ones that can work directly into the physical body; the highest are working down into the physical. We must not confuse physical with material. Man is an invisible being and he assembles material and thereby makes himself visible here on earth. Do not confuse that with the merely material substance, the matter that is gathered. The form which you maintain all through life is organizing the substance according to its own nature and its own law. It is not the substance that is building the form, the substance is passing through like a stream the whole time. We talk of catabolism, the breaking down, anabolism, the building up, and all that is going on in every cell of our body is metabolism. Every single cell has to be served, on the one hand, with the breath that it needs, and, on the other, with the substance that it needs, and then the removing of the waste products: every single cell of the body has to be served. So the highest spirits are called the Spirits of Strength, who can work right down into the physical body. Into that realm where we are most unawake, because we do not know what happens after we have had our food; unless there is something wrong with the food, or with us when we do not have the strength to digest it.

The next rank of spirits, the second hierachy as they are called, are able to work down into the life-forces. They are called Spirits of Light (Kyriotetes, Dynamis, Exusiai), where light is life. Without light there is no life, but what is light? You can never see it. You can see things illuminated but you can never see light. Rudolf Steiner speaks of it as a realm between the outwardly visible and the inwardly spiritual, it is a kind of mediating realm. It plays between substance and spirit, that is the etheric life.

Then the third group Rudolf Steiner calls Spirits of Soul. They enable us to co-ordinate our thoughts, feeling and will, within our consciousness. They are the third hierachy, the Angels,

Archangels and Archai that the teachers particularly have to relate to in their educational work.

The whole assumes a tremendous depth and without the farmer there can be no real education. Until we have farmers who really know what they are doing, we are not really giving people the bread of life. I remember Ehrenfried Pfeiffer and this true story which I had from him first-hand. He was travelling in a train with Rudolf Steiner to whom he was very closely connected as a young man. Rudolf Steiner even guided him personally in what he was to study. He was at the time a chemist. He had the temerity as a young man to say to Steiner, 'Why is it that more people do not develop the faculties that you speak of, Imagination, Inspiration, Intuition?' He had the courage to ask that, and he got an answer which was overwhelmingly unexpected – 'Food! Until you find the right nourishment that the body needs you cannot develop these spiritual faculties adequately.' So, in this question of food you are in the deepest realm. It is extraordinary how it has not penetrated sufficiently into our educational movement, because the teachers themselves have not realized it sufficiently. It means that you develop people of goodwill, but who lack Will, they cannot penetrate through. They remain with kind ideas and social feelings, they are nice people, they will not be bowled over by any sort of political movement, they have a certain amount of human stability. But it stops short of the realm of transformation. Will – the spiritual energy to transform! We live in the world of form, everything is formed – we are the only beings who can transform. Our life is measured by the degree of transformation we bring about. We can transform life for the better or worse, we can destroy it, but we can also build it up.

I feel that for a right education we need a combination of the enlightened *teacher*, of the *doctor* who is in his way an artist – it should be the artist who, through his work, is a doctor – and the *farmer and gardener*. We have talked about the village as a community in the past, and how that has disintegrated and vanished somehow. I have been dreaming of a new kind of village and I call it a village or community of gifts. Whenever I talk to people about to start a new school I tell them to get a piece of land first. 'Don't tie yourself up in buildings that later do not serve. Acquire a piece of land and put up any sort of buildings temporarily, anything that will do for a beginning, and then slowly build up what you require, but in any case begin with the piece of land.' I have said that in many parts of the world, and a few people have listened. In my community of gifts we need the land: *we must have the farm*, and in association with the farm there can grow up a school.

In association with these two you need a doctor. In the school you must have arts and crafts. If you have a school for normal children, then you should have a home-school for children who need special help, and cannot help themselves. I think you also need a rehabilitation centre, and a place where old people can live: and all these in relation to each other are a true injunction. 'Man know thyself, in body, soul and spirit.' If all these people share that thought in their different specialities – you have sculptors, painters, eurythmists, all the arts, speech and drama; a community of people in their different capacities and spheres of work, the one related to the other so that in their totality they build up a true image of what the human being can be – that is the new Spirit, you might say, that permeates the whole community.

Rudolf Steiner in the first Waldorf school's curriculum, in his advice to teachers, placed gardening in classes six, seven and eight (that is to say children of 12, 13 and 14 years of age, before they go into the high school). They are to have a garden and they are supposed to be able to go through a kind of three-year cycle at least. That was part of his picture, that all children should make contact with the soil and the plants and the flowers, should have an opportunity to sow a seed and watch it grow. Now, I wanted to extend this to the whole twelve classes. I think in every year of the child's twelve years at the Waldorf school there should be a period where they make active contact with Nature, and I have worked out something towards this with a school in Haarlemsville in America. We also had a meeting of the gardening teachers of the Waldorf schools in Great Britain and we drew up a kind of plan. In the Waldorf school you are touching different spheres of nature all the way through the curriculum, and

my recommendation was that the child in each year should make
a new contact with the world of nature around and with the soil,
and learn to know the animals, both domesticated and wild.

I think the whole Waldorf school curriculum has to be reviewed
from this aspect: we have to learn to love the Earth. We cannot
learn to love the Earth if we continue to think of it merely as a
clod of matter spinning mechanically around its own axis and the
Sun. That is one of the great illusions. We have really descended
to the Earth, we have our feet on the earth, but in our present day
we have lost the heavens. I think that the task of Biodynamic
agriculture is to relate once more the Earth to the world of the
stars, to the heavens.

I have finished with this picture, I cannot go more deeply into
it. But something was said this morning that I want to link onto.
In the Greek times we were under the sign of Aries the ram. It
was at that time that philosophy was born, the thought-life was
developed to a most marvellous degree. What is the sign we are
in now? Pisces, the fishes. If there was time, we would have to
go back and back, right to Lemuria, to the Fall, when man was
still invisible and, stage by stage, he had to enter into visibility,
enter more and more into matter. The culmination of this was
the perfect imagination of the beauty of the human form, and
it was then that Christ incarnated under Aries. Now we have
entered the phase of the fishes, a new beginning. Up to Aries,
all is incarnation, finding perfect expression in Greek art, Greek
philosophy, Greek drama, but from that time on we are in a
process of spiritualization. Up to the time of Christ the world was
still coming into being, now the world has begun to pass away
('The world will pass away, but my word will not pass away'.)
'My word' is the 'I AM'. So, I have the feeling that in this new
modern age we have bumped down heavily into matter and lost
the heavens: but now we are working out of the depths, not by
inspiration from above, but by giving birth within ourselves. We
have to find a new relationship with the Earth, we have to lead the
Earth back, through our inner activity, to find again a relationship
with the stars. Agriculture would then become a true agriculture,
a culture of the Earth.

In this way Biodynamic work can be seen as a tremendous step towards this transformation, towards this spiritualization. There are lots of people in Great Britain who are organic farmers, and carry their work with faithfulness and enthusiasm. However, they are still hanging on to a little of the old world. This further step to reach the stars from within is not the shining down from above, the old path of wisdom, but, as Steiner describes it, the ascent once again on the path of Will. It is in this connection that I see the special task of Biodynamic farming and gardening, for the strengthening of the Will, through the right treatment and the healing of the body. That is why there ought to be new villages and new communities arising around Biodynamic work: that is why we need teacher, doctor, farmer, working together as three good fellows, in service to the total nature of the human being. These are tremendous goals and we have to become choleric, even the most phlegmatic person has to begin to develop a fire in the belly. Without that, nothing can happen, other than bombs. That is the negative aspect of what should be happening: a fire born from within, a transforming fire. Instead of that we have annihilating forces. That is what we are up against. That has to be overcome.